Representing Sport

Representing Sport

ROD BROOKES
Lecturer in Media and Cultural Studies,
Cardiff University

A member of the Hodder Headline Group
LONDON
Co-published in the United States of America by
Oxford University Press Inc., New York

First published in Great Britain in 2002 by
Arnold, a member of the Hodder Headline Group,
338 Euston Road, London NW1 3BH

http://www.arnoldpublishers.com

Co-published in the United States of America by
Oxford University Press Inc.,
198 Madison Avenue, New York 10016

The advice and information in this book are believed to be true and
accurate at the date of going to press, but neither the author nor the publisher
can accept any legal responsibility or liability for any errors or omissions.

British Library Cataloguing in Publication Data
A catalogue entry for this book is available from the British Library

Library of Congress Cataloging-in-Publication Data
A catalog record for this book is available from the Library of Congress

ISBN 0 340 74051 5 (hb)
ISBN 0 340 74052 3 (pb)

1 2 3 4 5 6 7 8 9 10

Production Editor: James Rabson
Production Controller: Iain McWilliams
Cover Design: Terry Griffiths

Typeset in 11/14pt Sabon by Phoenix Photosetting, Chatham, Kent
Printed and bound in Great Britain by MPG Books Ltd, Bodmin, Cornwall

What do you think about this book? Or any other Arnold title?
Please send your comments to feedback.arnold@hodder.co.uk

Contents

Acknowledgements

I would like to thank the following for their friendship and support over the period of writing this book: Stuart Allan, Gill Branston, Daran Brookes, Cindy Carter, Peter Garrett, Sanna Inthorn, Sarah Knights, Justin Lewis and Terry Threadgold, as well as staff colleagues and research students in the School of Journalism, Media and Cultural Studies at Cardiff University. I would also like to thank Lesley Riddle at Arnold for her endless encouragement, patience and help, and Vanessa Mitchell for all her work on the final script.

The book is dedicated to my parents Chris and Pauline.

Abbreviations

ABC	American Broadcasting Company
AFL	American Football League
ATP	Association of Tennis Professionals
BBC	British Broadcasting Corporation
CART	Championship Auto Racing Teams
CBC	Canadian Broadcasting Corporation
CBS	Columbia Broadcasting Company
CTV	Canadian Television Network
ECW	Extreme Championship Wrestling
FA	Football Association (UK)
FIA	Fédération Internationale de l'Automobile
FIFA	Fédération Internationale de Football Association
GATT	General Agreement on Tariffs and Trade
IAAF	International Amateur Athletic Federation
IOC	International Olympic Committee
ISL	International Sport and Leisure
ITV	Independent Television Network (UK)
MLB	Major League Baseball
NBA	National Basketball Association
NBC	National Broadcasting Company
NFL	National Football League
NHL	National Hockey League
UEFA	European Football Association
USATF	United States Association of Track and Field
USOC	United States Olympic Committee

WCW	World Championship Wrestling
WLAF	World League of American Football
WNBA	Women's National Basketball Association
WTA	Women's Tennis Association
WWF	World Wrestling Federation
WTO	World Trade Organisation
XFL	WWF-owned Football League

|1|

Introduction

This book aims to examine the cultural and social significance of the increasingly important role of sport within a global media industry undergoing fundamental transformation. Sport appears to be ever more visible within the media. Live sports events have been crucial to the introduction of new pay television services. Sports stars provide a rich source of human interest for a news and entertainment industry in which celebrity and scandal stories in general are particularly newsworthy. Sports journalism has become a staple of rolling news channels on television and radio, and is already central to the business strategies of Internet content providers. To the extent that McLuhan's vision of a 'global village' (McLuhan and Fiore, 1967) enabled by electronic communications has been realised, the Olympic Games and the men's soccer World Cup are its major events.

The ways in which media companies have used sport to generate income and attract prestige have expanded and diversified, and, conversely, some sports organisations have benefited from the revenues that have accrued to the rights owners of popular events. The relationship between sport and the media has been described as 'symbiotic', based on mutual self-interest. Since the 1980s the boundaries between the two have become increasingly blurred. The intricacy of relationships between media and sport has been described by Jhally (1989) as a 'sports/media complex'. This book is based on the premise that this sports/media complex is playing an important role in the transformation of global mediated culture, and that the differ-ent implications of this development deserve investigation.

However, despite its self-evident importance as part of the major transformations affecting the media, sport still occupies a relatively marginal position within the academic fields that would seem to be responsible for addressing such issues: communication, cultural stud-ies and media studies. I would suggest that the reason that sport has been largely ignored is that it falls between two intellectual traditions that dominate thinking about the role of the media.

One tradition assesses the performance of the media according to how much it measures up to an ideal 'public sphere' role in providing the information citizens need to function in a democracy. From this perspective sport can play no more than a distracting role. Sport is often casually listed as one of a number of symptoms – alongside crime reconstructions, leisure and entertainment magazine pro-grammes, game and talk shows, and other supposedly 'trivial' forms – which are taken as indicators of the decline of the 'public service' model of broadcasting, a model which privileges its informational role (particularly news about politics and social issues) over enter-tainment. According to this view, modern sport is one of a number of highly commercialised entertainment forms driving out serious jour-nalism and increasingly inhibiting what the media should really be doing.

The second tradition evaluates the performance of the media as a form of popular culture, often, although not necessarily, from an explicitly postmodern perspective. According to this view, popular culture is not despised as mass distraction but rather celebrated as a means through which, for example, dominant ideologies can be sym-bolically resisted and marginalised identities asserted. Within this tradition sport is largely ignored, and understandably so. (The chief apologist for this tradition, Fiske, writes about sport only in relation to wrestling, of which more below.) Sports fandom is still predomi-nantly the preserve of one dominant group, men, and sport has undoubtedly functioned historically to reinforce stereotypical defini-tions of race and gender (see Chapters 5 and 6). From a cultural stud-ies perspective, the celebration of sport as popular culture is, to say the least, problematic, and it is not difficult to appreciate why it has therefore been largely ignored.

My argument is that the predominance of these two intellectual traditions has played a disabling role when it comes to analysing sport (and perhaps also other cultural practices that do not fit neatly within either paradigm). Thus while entrepreneurs like Rupert Murdoch appreciate the crucial importance of sport in developing new media markets, there is a real silence in media studies. Sport falls foul of the binary thinking that structures this divide between the traditions and sees, for example, rationality v. emotion, the public sphere v. private space, citizenship v. consumerism, information v. entertainment. For one tradition sport is a frivolous diversion from serious issues, for the other tradition sport doesn't fit easily into its particular definition of popular culture.

Nevertheless, there are indications that sport is beginning to be taken more seriously within media and cultural studies. Since I started writing this book two others on sport and the media have been published (Boyle and Haynes, 2000; Rowe, 1999). Further, it would be a mistake to conclude that because the subject has been largely ignored within media and cultural studies it has been ignored altogether in academic research. On the contrary, there is a substantial body of literature on media and sport within the sociology of sport, to be found in such journals as *International Review for the Sociology of Sport, Journal of Sport and Social Issues* and *Sociology of Sport Journal*. One of the aims of this book is to publicise this important research within a media and cultural studies context.

I would argue that media sport deserves greater attention within media and cultural studies on the basis that it foregrounds important issues around identity, culture, and politics. Analysis of the production, content and consumption of media sport raises key questions about the commodification and globalisation of culture, the construction of cultural and social identities and the role journalism plays in representing issues such as domestic violence and racism.

Further, the media are significantly transforming sport itself. As the importance of broadcast sport drives media companies to pay escalating prices for the more prestigious events and competitions, and as advertising and sponsorship account for an increasingly significant proportion of sports revenue, the implications for participants and fans alike are crucial. Commercialisation threatens to lead to increased polarisation between the rich and poor within individual sports, between different sports, and particularly between men's and women's sports, with all the implications for participation lack of resources entail. In the more lucrative sports, commercialisation promises to price traditional fans out of the market and to change the nature of the sports audience itself. At the same time globalisation threatens the viability of sport in smaller nations, weakening links between sport and place-defined cultural identities.

Political, technological and social change has explicitly rendered the binary oppositions problematic. Recent social theory has characterised present society using such labels as 'the risk society', 'the consumer society', etc., but from what can generally be described as a critical, 'late modern' perspective. This perspective is based on an understanding of the importance of the role of the post-Fordist or post-industrial economy in recent social change. It argues that sport has undergone a fundamental change over the last twenty years or so, which problematises 'modern' ways of thinking about the primacy of the public sphere over entertainment and requires us to take sport seriously, but at the same time rejects an interpretation of these changes as 'postmodern'.

If the role of the media in the transformation of sport as a cultural and social practice is to be understood, then we need a definition of what sport is. Typically studies of the relationship between media and sport begin with a discussion of historical and sociological accounts of how modern sport developed as a social practice (see for example Goldlust, 1987; Rowe, 1999). This book will differ in defining the culturally specific character of sport through a discussion of a televised physical contest which superficially shares many of the same characteristics as many sports, and is televised and marketed in similar ways, but in many ways represents the opposite of everything sport stands for: professional wrestling.

Wrestling v. sport

Wrestling is not a sport, it is a spectacle (Barthes, 1973: 15).

Lisa Simpson: You're sending us to a doctor who advertises on pro-wrestling?

Homer Simpson: Boxing, Lisa, boxing. There's a world of difference ('There's no disgrace like home', *Simpsons*, first broadcast 28 Jan 1990)

We might agree with Roland Barthes and Homer Simpson that wrestling is not a sport. But why not? – and what does that tell us about what sport is?

Wrestling has been transformed as television entertainment over the last few years. A major player in the transformation has been the World Wrestling Federation (WWF). The WWF was valued at $1bn when it sold shares to the public in 1999 ('Wrestling Federation sets its net worth at $1 billion', *New York Times*, 11. 9. 99). The previous financial year the WWF doubled its revenue from $126m to $251m, and increased its net income sixfold, from $8.5 to $56m ('Stock you can jump on – but look out for a fall', *Washington* Post, 4. 8. 99). Beginning with a deal with UPN, wrestling shows have become one of the most regularly watched cable programmes. Like many other successful media enterprises, WWF has based its success on differentially packaging the same product for different demographic markets.

One of the ways in which it does this is to present the same bout differently according to audience: the daytime WWF *Livewire* and *Superstars* avoid bad language and cut away from particularly violent-looking falls, while WWF *Raw is War*, a late-night version aimed at adult audiences, features female 'wrestling managers', often depicted through *Playboy*-style soft porn imagery. Viacom's intention to shift WWF *Heat*, which is packaged to specifically appeal to youth audiences, to MTV, further demonstrates this differential targeting ('Smackdown: Viacom wins USA's wrestling', *New York Times*, 28. 6. 00).

Another technique is to provide carefully designed 'soap opera' storylines which feature a huge cast of characters with differentiated appeal. WWF has, in particular, begun to target teenage (and even pre-teenage boys) through cross-promotion with the music, toy, magazine publishing, and video-game industries. In 2000 *Smackdown* was top of the all-format video game charts, even ahead of the phenomenonal *Pokémon*. WWF was regularly one of the most popular terms entered into search engines. A CD, *Aggression*, was released of the different wrestlers' entrance music, all in a generalised metal/hip-hop crossover style, by male rappers such as Run DMC, Ice T, and Ol' Dirty Bastard and Method Man of the Wu Tang Clan, guaranteed to exploit white teenage boys' fascination with black youth culture. WWF's most recognisable character, the Rock, author of best-selling autobiography *The Rock Says* (1998), appeared in a cameo in an episode of *Star Trek Voyager*, contributed a vocal to Wyclef Jean's single *It Doesn't Matter*, and was invited to introduce the House speaker at the 2000 Republican convention ('Pop culture extravangaza to replace ideological conventions of years past', *New York Times*, 31.7.00). Undoubtedly, WWF provides a textbook example of how a property can be aggressively exploited through marketing, licensing and cross-promotion (Frith, 1996).

WWF describes its product as 'sports entertainment', and wrestling is marketed in ways that associate it with sport. For example, in the UK during one week in April 2000, Murdoch's Sky TV was screening thirty hours of WWF in various packages, all but six of these hours on its subscription Sky Sports channels. Much of this was used to promote the *Insurrexion* pay-per-view event at London's Earls Court. WWF wrestling is seen as one of only a few types of event with the necessary must-see status to make it capable of being marketed on this basis, the others being boxing and pop concerts. Nevertheless, there was not a single reference to WWF wrestling on the sports pages of the comprehensive Sky website. This demonstrates the ambiguity of wrestling's relationship to sport: while it was a key part of Sky's strategy to build audiences for its sports channels, it was ignored by Sky's sports news department.

In general, wrestling rarely figures in newspaper sports sections, or sports news websites. Most academic texts on media and sport similarly ignore it, or mention it only in passing.

Yet wrestling involves many of the same characteristics as sport: it is based on a contest and involves performance based on strength, speed, agility and coordination. Indeed, superficially it seems to be closer to sports like boxing than boxing is to sports which value different combinations of human attributes and even technology. So why, unlike boxing, is it not classified as a sport?

The obvious answer is that the outcomes of wrestling bouts are arranged in advance. This is crucial – because the unpredictable unfolding of events is central to the character of sport, and explains, for example, the rigour with which sports organisations pursue match fixing, and (from a commercial viewpoint) concerns over the effect which a single dominant player or team could have on a sport. (For example, after his victory at the British Open in 2000 many newspapers were concerned about whether the dominance of Tiger Woods was good for golf as a spectacle.)

I would argue, however, that the difference between wrestling and sport is even more fundamental than the matter of the outcomes being arranged in advance, important though this aspect is. Wrestling, as Fiske pointed out (1989: 86; 1987), is a parody of sport, and this characterisation can be extended to cover the way wrestling parodies the regulation of space, time and conduct intrinsic to the development of modern sport. Before demonstrating this in detail, it is necessary to say something about the nature of modern sport and wrestling and how they became what they are.

Both are products of longer historical processes of economic, social and cultural transformation. Professional wrestling emerged at the same time as many of the important sports in the US and Europe, that is, from the mid to late nineteenth century. The historical emergence of professional wrestling was dependent on the historical emergence of sport in its modern form.

There have been various explanations of the emergence of modern sport. Malcolmson (1982) and others have argued that sport was part of the process of social control over working-class leisure. Elias argues that the formation of sport was part of a 'civilising process' through which the body and the emotions were both expressed and restrained (1986). Miller and McHoul (1998) have argued that sport represented an ideal apparatus for disciplining individual's bodies through, for example, physical training. What these accounts have in common is that they interpret the formation of modern sports as a means through which physical and emotional expression is encouraged whilst at the same time this expression is within societal limits. And it needs to be added that gender is central to understanding the disciplinary aspects of the formation of modern sport (Jenkins, 1997). On the one hand, sport regulated acceptable masculinity, based on fitness, and self-restraint. On the other hand, in the nineteenth century and for much of the twentieth, the exclusion of women from sport was justified by, and simultaneously reinforced, dominant ideologies that women were biologically unsuited for physical activity.

The formation of modern sport could be seen as an attempt both to *discipline* and *commodify* adult play. What it represented was the imposition of limits in terms of space, time and conduct. Firstly, the playing *spaces* of folk versions of football from the medieval period until the nineteenth century were determined by local geography. For example, in Dunning and Sheard's account of the game at Llanwennog in South Cardiganshire, Wales, the inhabitants were divided into the Bros occupying the high grounds of the parish, and the Blenaus, occupying the lowlands. The winners were those who got the ball to their end of the parish (1979: 29–30; see also Dunning, 1999: 83–93). By contrast, the development of modern soccer and rugby involved making the playing area uniform and fully observable by spectators. Secondly, the *duration* of medieval football was flexible. The Llanwennog game lasted as long as it took until the goal was reached: 'sometimes it would be dark before either party secured a victory'. By contrast, modern soccer and rugby imposed fixed time limits that were more consistent with the time-discipline of industrial capitalism. Finally, folk football often resulted in physical injuries and occasionally in death. At Llanwennog 'sometimes a kick on the shins would lead the two men concerned to abandon the game until they decided who was the better pugilist' (Dunning and Sheard, 1979: 29–30). By contrast, modern soccer and rugby distinguished between legitimate and illegitimate conduct. The introduction of an open, uniform playing area ensured that the conduct of participants could be scrutinised by officials and spectators alike, limiting the possibility of illegal behaviour against people and property. The formation of modern sport in the nineteenth century can be read as an attempt by national governments to discipline popular pursuits in order to maximise the economic efficiency of the population, to maintain social order, and to protect property rights.

However, as indicated above, the processes involved in the formation of modern sports were not just *disciplinary*, they also simultaneously worked to *commodify* sport. Just as the standardisation of sport according to the regulation of time, space and conduct, provided a method of social control through the regulation of popular leisure, it also produced a spectacle that could be sold to spectators through admission fees. In this way sport was part of a broader process of the commercialisation of popular culture from the end of the nineteenth century.

Most of the team sports that feature so strongly in the media were 'invented' during the second half of the nineteenth century. Since their formation, many have undergone rule changes to improve them as spectacles, particularly in recent times for the benefit of the television audience. Nevertheless the underlying structures have remained intact.

Returning to the idea of wrestling as a parody of sport, we can now examine how wrestling parodies the regulation of space, time and conduct intrinsic to the development of modern sport. As in sport, there is a demarcated space in which wrestling bouts apparently take place. But central to wrestling is the action that goes on *outside* the ring (such as 'illegal' blows meted out to wrestlers who fall out or are thrown out of the ring by opponents and their allies, antics by managers or tag team partners to distract the referee from illegal acts carried outside the ring, the use of metal steps to inflict physical damage). This action outside the ring is central to the development of feuds and to establishing the characters of good guys ('faces') or bad guys ('heels'). Indeed, in WWF much of the action takes place backstage, or even in the car park, and increasingly relies on television cameras to convey the narrative to the audience in the arena and at home. Whereas in most sports the arena is clearly demarcated and separated off, wrestling is based around a *transgression* of the demarcated space in which the bout is supposed to take place, i.e. the ring.

As in sports, the contest is supposed to unfold until one party has achieved supremacy, and might be won by overall dominance or through a surprise turnaround at the end. But in wrestling the outcome is arranged in advance and generally follows a number of set plots: for example, the hero who prevails; the bad guy who wins, but only through cheating, and who gets his comeuppance in a later bout.

As in other sports, there is a set code of conduct to regulate acceptable versus unacceptable methods of combat. So, too, there is a referee who oversees contests in order to ensure that codes of conduct are followed, and who is responsible to the governing body. But in the case of wrestling the referee is frequently knocked out or distracted. Referees are verbally and even physically abused by commentators and wrestlers, and are also disciplined or dismissed by the company. Bouts are regularly won through illegal holds, or won as the result of blows meted out outside the ring, possibly by other wrestlers.

One of the characteristics of the formation of the modern sports was the separation of participants from spectators. But in WWF there is a host of characters who are not wrestlers who are involved in an ongoing soap opera. The promoters are involved as characters. The WWF has been owned by the McMahon family, but now the owners have become participants. Vince McMahon, the 'real' chief executive of the WWF also plays the character of Vince McMahon, the evil promoter, directly intervening in bouts from the ringside, fixing referees and bookers to ensure victories for his tame stable of wrestlers. Other characters in this dysfunctional family include the 'meddling wife', Linda, the bosses' son, Shane, and the daughter Stephanie, who is 'married' to one of the WWF superstars, 'Triple H' aka 'the Game'. Storylines are constructed around the ever-shifting alliances within this family.

The on-screen soap opera represents a distorted version of off-screen events involving the WWF. In 2001 the WWF bought its rival the WCW (World Championship Wrestling). On screen during this time, the acquisition was used as a basis for a power struggle within the McMahon family between Vince and his son Shane, who became chair of the WCW, and Stephanie, who is chair of the smaller ECW (Extreme Championship Wrestling), culminating in a pay-per-view event between the various stables of wrestlers.

The whole point is that in mainstream sports the administrators are supposed to be neutral, representing the sport as a whole or if not, the interests of competing teams in an even-handed manner. In wrestling they are corrupt, dispensing favours.

Furthermore, since 1977, when Jenkins wrote that there were only two women in the WWF universe, the number of women has increased dramatically. As the role of many of these women is to provide the type of voyeuristic glamour associated with *Sports Illustrated* swimsuits calendars, or even *Playboy*, they have to feature as 'managers', rather than as wrestlers, as the latter would involve the type of muscle development that doesn't easily fit with the codes of conventional glamour imagery. Women are now central to many of the soap opera storylines featured on the WWF programmes, with jealousies, insults, etc. providing the reason for many of the feuds. Thus, despite not being wrestlers these females are involved in the action, cheating to aid their partners, or being 'unwillingly' drawn in.

Even television coverage of wrestling represents a parody of the usual conventions of television sport. A convention that has developed in commentary is the division of labour between the commentator and the summariser (in the USA, between play-by-play and colour announcer), who is often an ex-athlete. The former's expertise lies in calling the action, the latter's in contextualising it (see Chapter 2). The convention is that both remain neutral, although this is usually waived in the case of national broadcasters covering events in which their national team is competing against another nation. By contrast, in television wrestling the commentators are effectively colour announcers with antagonistic sympathies. They sit at the side of the ring but are often involved in the action, their table or monitors used to inflict damage. Regularly, commentators like WWF's King will get involved in the ring itself.

Wrestling is a spectacle of excessive and thoroughgoing rule-breaking: rule-breaking that is not just occasional, it's the whole point – wrestling makes no sense without it. Wrestling appears at first sight to have the same type of rules governing the playing area, and the duration and conduct of the contest as mainstream sports. Yet it works by breaking all those rules.

Fiske uses wrestling as an example of how popular culture should not be seen as an instrument of social control, as a means through which dominant ideologies are imposed on docile mass audiences. He argues that in wrestling the carnivalesque aspects work to subvert the imposition of rules and authority from above through parody. In this respect, he suggests, wrestling is different from sport. For Fiske, wrestling 'exaggerates certain elements of sport so that it can question both them and the values that they normally bear. It recovers the offensive popular pleasures that the nineteenth-century bourgeoisie struggled so hard to appropriate and make respectable' (Fiske, 1989: 96). By implication, sport does operate as an apparatus of social control. Sport is only of relevance insofar as, by comparison, it demonstrates the subversiveness of wrestling.

If wrestling represents a parody of sport by transgressing and inverting sport's deeply held values, equally the guardians of mainstream sports work diligently to distance their sports from what wrestling represents. This is particularly evident in boxing, where the superficially similar nature of the sport, its commercial exploitation, and insinuations of criminality amongst promoters, have exposed boxing to accusations that it is becoming like professional wrestling. The humour in Homer Simpson's naïve insistence that there is a 'world of difference' between boxing and professional wrestling relies on the viewers suspecting that there isn't. It is perhaps significant that some of the bad guys and girls of various sports flirted with wrestling at particular moments in their careers. When the Nevada State Athletic Commision suspended 'baddest man on the planet'

Mike Tyson for biting Evander Holyfield's ear, Tyson appeared as a 'special enforcer' at WWF's *Wrestlemania XIV* in March 1998. After figure skater Tonya Harding was banned for her part in having Nancy Kerrigan's knee whacked, she later appeared as a wrestling manager, and was herself invited to wrestle by Japanese promoters, but declined. Basketball player Dennis Rodman, whose autobiography was called *Bad as I Wanna Be* (Rodman and Keown, 1997), fought in WCW wrestling under the name 'Rodzilla'.

Thus the relationship of wrestling to mainstream sports is widely held to be related but distinct. Wrestling depends on the distinctive values of mainstream sport to parody, mainstream sports distinguish themselves from everything that wrestling represents. But are there signs that the boundaries between sport and wrestling are becoming less and less clear?

In early 2001, WWF launched an eight-city, eight-team football tournament branded XFL. This contest was aimed at audiences alienated by the increasing tendency in AFL, as in many mainstream sports, to regulate violent conduct so as to protect what are increasingly becoming expensive commercial properties from the risk of long-term injury. Instead, XFL promised to restore the qualities of 'real football' – arguably the same values that underpin WWF. Yet XFL was classified as a sport, albeit one in which a television company – NBC – has invested $30bn at the outset, in order to run a twelve-week Saturday night prime-time season ('Pro wrestling, NBC hope to produce gripping product; XFL football is ready to rumble', *Washington Post*, 2.5.00). It was announced that the rules of XFL would be changed to speed up the game, player celebrations would be encouraged, kit would be relaxed and microphones would be everywhere to pick up the 'trash talk' (which would be positively encouraged). Once the season started, cameras and interviewers were allowed into dressing rooms in order to develop the personalities of the players. There were glamour model cheerleaders. In other words, WWF used many of the presentational methods familiar from pro-wrestling (building up soap opera storylines around interpersonal conflicts, etc.), while at the same time maintaining the integrity of the sport.

However, by the end of its first season XFL was disbanded. During its season it had delivered the lowest prime-time ratings of any of the four networks. It lost XFL and NBC $35m each ('McMahon, NBC announce disbandment of XFL', *ESPN.COM* 10 May 2001). XFL perhaps provides an interesting lesson about the limits to the commercial exploitation of sport. Despite employing all the resources and experience of one of the world's most successful entrepreneurial companies, the failure of XFL demonstrates that sports fans' interest cannot simply be bought through expensive marketing.

About this book

This book is structured on the premise that something fundamental has been happening to sport over the last twenty years or so, epitomised by the recent example of the launch of XFL, and that the media has played a key role in this transformation. This has implications for the ways in which we consider the cultural and social significance of sport.

Chapter 2 examines the different means through which sport is represented in the media. It focuses on two different aspects of media coverage: sport as a media event, and sports (and sport-related) journalism. Sport as a live media event is crucial to the economic and cultural value of major sports to television. Traditionally, broadcasters have tended to combine a journalistic approach to recording sports events in which the television viewer is located in the ideal spectator position at the event. Typically, the means through which sport events are recorded are not made explicit. With increasing commercialisation, there are signs that new technological developments and presentational techniques are changing what has been a fairly conventionalised fixed televisual language. And as we have noted, spectators at a WWF event now depend on live behind-the-scenes coverage transmitted on the screen within the arena without which they would miss the continuing storylines that explain why particular feuds are taking place. While it would be wrong to suggest that there is a direct equivalent to this at sports events in terms of screens being used to communicate vital information to spectators at the event, television viewers are increasingly privileged to behind-the-scenes views, for instance shots from the locker-room. And presentational techniques are also used to provide an equivalent of wrestling's soap opera storylines: NBC's coverage of the 1996 Olympics, was – rather stereotypically – designed to appeal to women viewers through use of soap opera techniques.

At the same time there has been expansion and diversification of journalism covering sport. This is reflected not just in the increase in sports news content, but also in greater coverage of sports politics and of scandals relating to sports personalities. There is more coverage of sport as an important public policy area, and more financial news about the sports industry. In many ways, scandal stories about sports personalities supply narratives analogous to the soap opera themes which build feuds in WWF. Chapter 2 discusses these different types of coverage.

Apart from the representational aspect of media sports coverage, which will be a central theme in this book, there is another aspect of the changing media–sport relationship that is crucial: the active role the media play in transforming sport through its commodification and globalisation. Chapter 3 examines the economic, political and cultural implications of the processes involved. Firstly, it discusses the changing economic character of the media–sport relationship, which it characterises as one of post-industrialisation, with increasing convergence between media and sport organisations. Secondly, it examines the politics of FIFA and the IOC (the governing body of the men's soccer World Cup and the International Olympic Committee) as they pursue similar strategies of encouraging globalisation through the commercial exploitation of media rights and sponsorship. Thirdly, it examines the cultural implications of globalisation and commercialisation, which problematise simplistic equations of economic strength with cultural power. There is a fissure between North American sporting culture and that of the rest of the world, which makes it difficult for economically powerful North American media and sports organisations to simply impose sports on places used to other sporting cultures. Although they have had some successes, recent attempts to market US football, basketball, baseball and hockey have met with uneven and partial success in other parts of the world, the degree of take-up depending entirely on the character of local sporting culture.

Discussion of the media's role in the globalisation and commodification of sport raises issues around sport's role in the formation of cultural and social identities. The rest of the book examines by turns the sports media's role in the construction of national, gendered and ethnic identities, emphasising the connections between these different types of identity. While it is widely accepted that media coverage of sport plays a role in reinforcing a sense of national identity, it seems to be the most explicitly stereotypical images that command attention – for example, jingoistic or xenophobic presentation of international sporting contests in the English tabloid press – at the expense of the way that the media encourage viewers and readers to identify with the national community in everyday, routine ways. We could for example examine the ways in which some WWF wrestlers fit in to crude stereotypes - (Jenkins, 1997: 73). By contrast, Chapter 4 seeks to examine the more complex ways in which the sports media contribute to the construction of national identity, particularly through television events like the Super Bowl. Of course, one of the principal objections to an analysis of the cultural and social implications of changes affecting the sports media is that these will relate predominantly to about half of the population, that is, since participation in and consumption of sport remains predominantly male. Whilst accepting a degree of male dominance in sport this book is based on an assumption that there is no reason why this should always be the case. Indeed the market-led strategies pursued by media and sports organisations seem to be having complex and contradictory effects. On the one hand, as young male audiences are targeted ever more aggressively, stereotypical 'glamour' images abound in the promotion of sport, particularly motor sport. On the other hand as marketers seek to find ways of exploiting what they see as a huge undeveloped market for sport – women – the presentation of events (as for example in NBC's coverage of the 1996 Atlanta

Olympics) might have effects on the types of representation on offer. These issues are discussed in Chapter 6.

The issue of 'race' is particularly visible in the sports media, which have been notable for more positive representations of black people than are typical of general media coverage in western societies, which tends to marginalise black people or present them negatively. However, these apparently positive images can be used to provide support for the argument that there is an essential, biological racial difference between black and white people. Conversely, on the occasion that black sports stars fall from grace through use of drugs or through their conduct in or out of the sports arena, this contrast between the Olympian ideal of sport and their behaviour seems to be amplified through quite stereotypical representations of race. Chapter 6 is based on the assumption that 'race' is constructed, and that the sports media play an important role in this construction. Apart from supplying a critique of this construction, this chapter also indicates the difficulties in discussing 'race', given its complexity – a key indicator of which is the significance that some black sports stars, not just those like Dennis Rodman and Charles Barkley whose media personae has been based on being 'bad', but also 'role models' like Michael Jordan, assume for young men, black and white. To touch again on a topic mentioned earlier, the use of black hip-hop style of music is not confined to WWF (wrestlers' entrance music); this style is used more widely to modernise sports presentation.

One of the pitfalls of exploring fundamental social identities like race or gender is the tendency to focus on either one of them to the detriment of other important social identities. If we are to analyse media representations of the rise and fall of Ben Johnson or the late Florence Griffith-Joyner, in both cases we need to foreground how their individual media personae fit with social identities around 'race', nation and gender.

Finally, a note of caution. This book is intended to identify the key *general* issues affecting the relationship between media and sport globally. Yet the pleasures that sport involves, those that make it such a valuable commodity, are ones that are deeply embedded in the personal and collective memories of individuals and communities (to some extent, this might explain why the USA has not been able to sell its major league sports across the whole world in the way that it does its films, pop music and television). As an illustration of the emotional attachment that sport has for its fans, in writing this book it was very difficult for me to use the word 'soccer' to describe the sport I've always known and loved as football – the word 'soccer' is hardly ever used in the UK. Nevertheless, in writing for an international readership, I've had to use the word to differentiate it from the US and Australian versions of football. This book seeks to identify and explore key themes and issues in media and sport internationally, but in writing it I hope to open up avenues for further research on how the themes and issues discussed are played out in specific national and local contexts.

2

Mediating sport

This chapter addresses an issue that is crucial to understanding the significance of the changes affecting the relationship between the media and sport: the question of how sport is mediated. The deconstruction of popular cultural texts such as soap opera and film through visual, textual and narrative analysis has now become commonplace within communication, cultural and media studies. Yet there has been less interest in analysing the ways in which sport is represented in the media. It is easy to speculate on the reasons for this. Television coverage of sports events has traditionally relied on tried and tested broadcasting conventions that have been developed precisely in order *not* to draw the viewers' attention away from the action. Sports journalism is often treated, within news organisations and universities alike, as trivial compared to political or war journalism. That said, an attempt to understand the media's significance in relation to sport involves, as in any other area of media studies, analysing the different ways in which sport is represented to its audiences through different formats. We need to look at the different institutional practices and professional ideologies through which sport is represented, study the complex ways in which audiences for media sport are constituted and addressed. Understanding these issues is all the more necessary because there are (and always have been) conflicts about how sport should be represented in the media. Some examples of the conflicts that will be discussed in this chapter are as follows:

1. Should television coverage of sports events should be as unintrusive as possible to give the viewer an experience analogous to attending an event in person? Or should it actively build the entertainment element through camera movement, rapid editing and computer graphics?
2. Should sports journalism concern itself only with matters directly related to sport, e.g. reports, news about injuries or player transfers? Or should journalists investigate how politics and business affect what happens in sports, events, and write about scandals relating to the private lives of sports stars?
3. Should it be assumed that the audience for media sport consists predominantly of committed sports fans, knowledgeable about sport, or should coverage be aimed at the general viewer or reader?

In practice these conflicts tend to be resolved in sports broadcasting and journalism: thus sports television presentation both conveys a sense of realism and introduces entertainment values; journalism about sport covers not just stories directly related to what happens on the field of play, but also on the politics, business and scandals of sport; and both sports broadcasters and journalists seek to cater for the committed fan while also aiming to broaden the audience.

But at a time when commodification and globalisation promise to fundamentally change media sport (see Chapter 3), it is worth considering how the ways in which these conflicts have traditionally been resolved might be affected. Will the commodification of television sport necessarily lead to faster editing, flashier graphics, proliferating camera positions, and increased interactivity, even to the extent of changing the rules of sports to make them more 'television-friendly'? Will market-led journalism inevitably submerge the traditional values of sports journalism under a proliferation of scandals? And what will be the role of the internet in both broadcasting (or perhaps more accurately narrowcasting) live and recorded sport, and as a journalistic medium?

In order to begin to address these questions we need to understand the complexity of the ways in which sport is currently mediated. The first section of the chapter examines the conventions governing how sports events are broadcast to audiences. The second section looks at what I would suggest are two different, and often conflicting, types of journalism about sport: news journalism, as it focuses on sports-related scandals as well as the politics and business of sport; and sports journalism itself, which should be considered a specialist form of journalism, with a distinctive professional culture and hierarchy of news values.

To some extent, this chapter will follow the standard practice in media, communication and cultural studies of addressing separately the production, content and consumption of media sport texts. However, while it makes sense to examine the production and content of sports broadcasting, sports journalism and sports-related journalism in different sections, the audience for these different types of media representation is effectively the same. Hence the audience for both sports broadcasting and sports journalism will be discussed in a third section. Although this section comes last, perceptions of the composition of the audience for media sport and how audience members use the media is crucial to the organisation of production and of the texts themselves, and will be referred to throughout. An understanding of the heterogeneous composition of the audience, and the different contexts in which fans and general viewers or readers consume media sport (whether individually or collectively, for example) is crucial for any speculation about how media sport will change.

Producing television sport

You can tell a bad sports production when you notice the production itself. . . the trick is, for me, when you don't notice the show . . . you feel like you're there . . . your interest is kept up all the time . . . [and] you're not aware of any of the production values. You're just glued to the set (Canadian Broadcasting

Corporation programme director interviewed in Gruneau, 1989: 143).

This apt and succinct summary of the ideal broadcast, from a producer's point of view, makes television sports production sound very simple. But as Gruneau (1989) and MacNeill (1996) show, sports production is a distinctive and complex type of television production based on considerable investment in personnel and technology. The deceptively simple aspirations of making the viewer feel that they're there, of gluing them to the set, mask complex production processes through which the demands of 'realism' and entertainment are reconciled.

Sports departments are required to produce much greater output than other television departments, under formidable pressures (Tunstall, 1993: 65). Like sports journalism, sports units are rationally organised to fulfil this requirement, with a hierarchical division of labour, typically between the producer, the director, commentators, camera operatives, vision and sound mixers, and technicians. Each individual has clearly defined responsibilities, which they are expected to fulfil despite any deficiencies in equipment (MacNeill, 1996: 110). Each is employed in a particular role according to skills and previous experience, although flexibility is also a desired quality. The pressures involved are not just of time but also of uncertainty, in that producers have to react to unpredictable occurrences both within the event and external to it.

An extreme instance of the former is how to cover death on the screen (Tunstall, 1993: 73). In late October 1999 broadcasters (Fox in the US, TSN in Canada and Eurosport) built up the last race in the Indy CART series as a championship showdown between Dario Franchitti and Carlos Montoya. But the popular young Canadian driver Greg Moore was fatally injured in a spectacular crash early in the race. Immediately decisions had to be made about whether to show replays within the broadcast, given the obvious seriousness of the crash. Then, unusually, Moore's death was announced to the viewers before the end of the race (which the organisers decided not to abandon), although the drivers were not told. The commentators were faced with the challenge of how to report the rest of the race, given that for many fans what remained had become an empty ritual. Finally viewers were faced with what appeared to be a very heartless gesture: the sight of winner Adrian Fernandez pumping the air with his fists in celebration. Of course, viewers did not know that he was unaware of what had happened.

More mundanely, directors are often faced with the problem of how to handle invasions of the sports arena by fans, demonstrators or 'streakers'. Sports producers even need to anticipate challenges posed by the weather: to position cameras to avoid shooting into the sun (Gruneau, 1989: 142), or to compensate for extreme contrasts of sun and shade where part of the playing area is in a stadium's deep shadow on a sunny day.

In response to the unpredictability of such events, conventional procedures have been derived based on lessons learned from past experience. For example, the response to spectator invasions of the playing area in the UK is to cut away to a long shot, a convention that developed after it become apparent that television coverage seemed to be encouraging such incursions through the promise of publicity.

The demands of live broadcasting require those working in sports television to develop distinctive skills: during live events editing has to be performed by directors, commentators have to talk unscripted. The production crew need to be able to work under pressure, be flexible and use their previous experience (Gruneau, 1989: 142). One sports producer in the UK has described his frustrations with the routine:

> A lot of hard work goes into it, but you have no say over most of
> its content ... As far as game coverage goes, it's just a question of
> having enough cameras so that you don't miss a tackle or an
> elbow off the ball ... Some people work 40 weeks of the year on
> a single programme ... It makes you very good at it, but it's not
> something I'd like to do (Rupert Rumney in Holland, 1997: 147).

In her study of CTV (Canadian Television Network) coverage of the 1988 Calgary Winter Olympics hockey tournament, MacNeill (1996: 111) found that most of the crew were not conscious of how the various telecast elements – auditory, verbal and visual – were culturally chosen in the past and slowly adapted to meet the needs of the changing needs of this network. Only the senior producers . . . admitted that CTV's 'Canadian' style of coverage was but one choice of many different stances available.

According to MacNeill, then, there is an occupational distinction in the hierarchy of labour between the few responsible for the overall look of the sportscast, aware of how sports broadcasting was 'swiftly conventionalised in the 1950s' and how these conventions have been modified, and the majority who are responsible for particular tasks, such as camerawork, who have come to see their particular craft as 'natural' and 'universal'.

The apparently fixed conventions of sports broadcasting developed in a relatively short space of time in the late 1940s and 1950s, and these conventions have been modified to meet changing economic and technological circumstances. The first moments of live television sports coverage – in the UK in 1937, a Wimbledon tennis match; in the US in 1939, a college baseball game using one camera giving a point of view along the third base line – were obviously relatively crude and were viewed by a few affluent viewers. After the interruption to production caused by the Second World War, US and UK broadcasters established the procedures that have since come to be taken for granted. From the beginning, these conventions were formulated to reconcile conflicting tensions:

The tension between 'realism' and entertainment. Realism is, in fact, the product of conventions. Whannel notes how for early BBC sports producers it was essential that the action was shot from one side of an imaginary line running between, or at right angles to, the key features of the playing area (for example, the goals in a soccer match, or the net in tennis) so as not to disorientate the viewer (Whannel, 1992: 32). British television sport conventions were developed:

to offer an apparently unmediated version of events and to establish points of viewer identification with recognisable star personalities. The representation is a product of the need to hold on to the transparency effect whilst building in entertainment value. (Whannel, 1992: 36–7).

The tension between providing for the general viewer or the sports fan. How can the need for accessibility be reconciled with offering specialist expertise? Crucial to this was the perception of the audience, which could be seen variously as consisting of the general sports fan, the fan of individual sports, or the member of the wider public, interested mainly in big events. Audience building required appealing to a range of different viewers.

According to Whannel, these potentially conflicting priorities have been reconciled in what have become standard procedures. For example, the convention has developed of combining professional commentators, who are employed because of their skills in conveying the game in an accessible way, with experts, usually former participants, who are able to give expert views on the subject.

An obvious aspect of television production is the imbalance between men and women employed in it. Gruneau's study (1989: 141, 143) of the CBC's coverage of the 1986 Whistler Downhill revealed that the production crew of 52 included only three women. The occupational culture of sports television production has a significant part in this gender imbalance. It inevitably involves location work, which requires travel away from home. A male-dominated culture is almost inevitable, given these requirements, and it is one in which banter reinforces the norm that television sports production is predominantly the preserve of men. MacNeill found that there was an assumption amongst the crew that women were not 'serious' fans of the game – although, as she points out, this was not based on any market research (1996: 116).

The gender imbalance characterises all aspects of production. The 1996 RTNDF/Ball State study of 679 US television stations revealed that only 3 per cent of sports anchors were women. Further, this imbalance seems to manifest itself at an early stage. A survey of two university schools of broadcast journalism in the USA showed that whereas 32 per cent of male students wanted to be broadcast play-by-play announcers, no female student held this aspiration. The balance was slightly more even between those students hoping to become television sports anchors or reporters: 19 per cent men, 8 per cent women (Tuohey, 1999: 39, 41). That female students seem to have ruled out play-by-play as a career aspiration at this early stage is significant. Where women are noticeably more visible as presenters, reporters and, on women's sports, colour announcers or summarisers, the almost complete absence of female play-by-play announcers tends to reinforce male voices as natural.

What changes does commodification entail for the production of television sport? Back in the early 1990s a UK television sports producer complained that his job was less about making programmes and more about 'contracts, management of people, budgets, planning and scheduling' (Tunstall, 1993: 71). In April 2000 the Head of BBC Sport resigned after having attracted media criticism over the BBC's loss of rights to a number of key sporting events (*Observer*, 16 April 2000). Sports television production has always been about doing the best possible job within economic and technical constraints, but a more competitive approach has developed, based on the need to balance costs against the benefits of increased prestige and greatest possible revenue. This is one way in which economic factors can affect the ways in which sports appear on screen. The number of cameras used to screen a prestigious event reinforces the importance of that event – less prestigious events are likely to be covered by a smaller number of cameras. For example, there may well be coverage of women's sports on the new specialist sports channels that will, it could be argued, provide important exposure and revenue for those sports. At the same time, the level of investment limits the ways in which such events will be represented: the number of cameras used, etc.

Economic factors increasingly mean that sports producers don't just cover a prestigious live event, they also promote it. Promotion means not only the inevitable trailers and advertisements but the coverage of the actual event itself. As the cost of acquiring rights to sports coverage escalates, such rights are increasingly treated as properties that need to be looked after. For commercial broadcasters, promotion of sports events is not only a matter of maximising revenue; it also boosts prestige. When it is time to negotiate new contracts, revenue isn't the only concern for sports organisations: the ways in which broadcasters have promoted the sport, or promise to promote the sport, is also important. When the BBC lost the rights to home cricket test matches to a partnership of Sky and Channel 4, the England and Wales Cricket Board was influenced not just by the increased revenue but by the innovative techniques they had been promised by Sky and Channel 4 to promote the game, particularly to younger audiences (Mitchell and Brooks, 1998). Channel 4's coverage now features a 'snickometer': by detecting the faintest of sounds this device is able to detect when the ball has hit the bat – important when there are disputed decisions on catches and leg before wicket.

Analysing televised sport

At its best, sport provides one of the most powerful forms of human drama on television, inviting an intense emotional involvement from its audience. Dramatic sporting moments justify the ever-higher price that broadcasters are prepared to pay for covering major competitions, not just in order to generate revenue through advertising and pay-TV, but also to gain or retain prestige. Multinational corporations are prepared to pay increasingly hefty fees to be associated with such events. Of course, sport in its recorded form also provides cheap routine filler for the proliferating specialist sports channels, but it is in the live events that makes television sport so significant.

Yet of course this intense emotional experience of watching television sport has to be produced. While they're watching, committed fans are unlikely to be aware of technical conventions regarding camera positioning, camera movement and editing, if the production achieves it intended effect of transparency. Indeed, the intensity of fans' involvement with the action depends on not being distracted by intrusive techniques.

In media and cultural studies television is often analysed using the concept of genre. This concept is based on the idea that within different kinds or types of television, there are common codes and conventions that are 'recognised and shared' by television producers and audiences (Creeber, 2001: 1). In analysing sports television using the concept, it is important to recognise that sports television does not constitute a single genre, but rather a mix of different forms of television production practice. Firstly, television coverage of major sporting contests belongs to the category of *media events* (Dayan and Katz, 1992) alongside royal weddings and funerals, state occasions, live music concerts, sometimes sharing the same outside broadcast production facilities (Tunstall, 1993). Secondly, the news reports, interviews and discussion panels that are integral to television sports broadcasts represent a specialised form of *journalism*, framed by a distinctive set of news values shared with newspaper and radio sports journalism. Finally, aspects of sports television often perform an explicitly *promotional* role. Title sequences and video segments promote sporting events through constructing narrative conflicts between participants, using techniques that are similar to those used in advertisements, pop videos and movie trailers.

The first live television sports events were broadcast before the Second World War – in the UK the first event was a Wimbledon tennis match in 1937, in the US a college baseball game at Columbia University in 1939 (Barnett, 1990: 5, 19). But it wasn't until the late 1940s and 1950s that the conventions of sports television that we now take for granted were established. For stadium-based events, in general, television presentation of many sports events continues to follow the rules of the 180° system: cameras are all positioned on one side of an imaginary line running from one end of the playing area to the other, as if to transgress this rule would disorientate the viewer. The coverage of the action is anchored by a main camera position that situates television viewers in the ideal spectator position. This camera position is fixed, and the camera pans, tilts and zooms following the action, cutting to medium-range shots at moments when the action is condensed into a small area. These cameras appear to give a view of the action that corresponds closely to what a spectator would ideally be able to see at the venue. During breaks in the action close-ups are cut with slow motion action replays and/or close-ups of the reactions of players or athletes, coaches and fans, inviting identification by the viewer. Presentational techniques have changed over the years: faster editing, the use of more camera positions and the introduction of new camera technologies (mobile, tracking, miniature and blimp cameras, for example), computer-generated graphics, animations, virtual reality reconstructions, aerial shots, etc. But whatever presentational innovations there have been over the years – the basic conventions for televising sport have remained constant.

Sports television is based on universally shared conventions, because the logistics of covering international sports events effectively demand a system in which a domestic national broadcaster provides a 'clean feed' and 'natural sound' for other national broadcasters to use as the basis for their presentation. International sports organisations like FIFA and the IOC encourage broadcasters to provide feed that will be universally accepted. For the 1978 men's soccer World Cup, held in Argentina, the host nation's broadcaster was persuaded by the EBU (European Broadcasting Union) to change their use of camera positions to give the style of coverage more acceptable to European viewers (Whannel, 1992: 166).

In analysing the visual content of sports television it is important to recognise the ways in which decisions about how to present sports events have implications for the representation of national identity, gender and 'race'. For example, fights have become an intrinsic part of hockey – yet broadcasters can differ in the way in which they represent these. MacNeill reports how Canadian broadcaster CTV carried coverage of fights as part of its responsibility to cover news aspects of games, whilst French language broadcaster TVA would cut to advertisements (1996: 114). The use of 'beauty shots' (MacNeill, 1996: 116) or 'honey shots' (Barnett, 1995: 165) – lengthy shots of attractive female spectators during breaks in the action – can also work to reinforce the perception that sport is a predominantly male activity.

Following radio, the conventions of television commentary have also developed to respond to uncertainty in the action. Commentary is organised around a division of labour between a commentator (UK)/play-by-play announcer (US), and a summariser (UK)/colour announcer (US). Typically, the former is an expert narrator, who takes responsibility for controlling the commentary, while the latter is an ex-athlete, who provides a participant's perspective. Although commentators can and do prepare extensive background notes, sports commentary represents a space for unscripted talk that has few parallels in the rest of television. In the case of live transmission of the men's soccer World Cup, for example, the host nation's broadcaster is responsible for visuals and natural sound whilst domestic broadcasters supply their own commentary. In anchoring the meaning of events for listeners and viewers, television commentary provides important material for the analysis of the social implications of television sport. To take two different examples: the improvised nature of commentary can lead to both unthinking and conscious national and racist stereotyping, while the accepted conventions of sports commentary (pitch and tone of voice, use of ex-players as experts) reinforce male dominance in these occupations, as noted earlier. Paralleling television presentation, entertainment values are becoming increasingly predominant in commentary, with some radio and television commentators and summarisers becoming stars in their own right.

Sports television also represents a form of journalism. Much of the content of sports telecasts is in the form of reports and interviews conducted by sports journalists before, during and after the event itself. As will be discussed in more detail below, sports journalism is a specialised branch of journalism with its own distinctive hierarchy of news values: focusing on such stories as disciplinary issues, contract negotiations between stars and teams, the levels of motivation and commitment of the stars, management tactics, injuries, etc.

Finally, sports television also performs a promotional role. Given that they have to recoup the escalating costs of sports rights, it isn't enough for broadcasters to only cover events, they also have to aggressively promote them. Title sequences and video segments typically set the scene for television coverage of major sporting events through using a variety of post-production techniques. The use of spectacular slow motion sequences, dramatic sound effects, eye-catching computer-generated graphics, theatrical music and voiceover all contribute to the construction of narrative conflicts between the participants to be resolved in the contest to follow. When sports television promotion plays this role in building up a sense of antagonism between different nations, there are implications for how national identities are represented (see Chapter 4).

The promotional role of sports television is equally crucial for public service broadcasters (who need to attract high ratings to justify the public's expenditure on acquiring expensive sports rights), commercial free-to-air broadcasters (who need to build audiences to sell to advertisers), and pay-TV or pay-per-view broadcasters (who have to persuade viewers to subscribe to their services).

Although sports television can be described as a *hybrid genre*, in practice it is impossible to identify clear boundaries between the different televisual practices that constitute it. A major live sports broadcast will typically follow seamlessly from the titles to an opening video segment, then a news report on the teams or individuals involved, then perhaps to a pre-event ceremony, then to expert discussion panels, into the game proper, and, lastly, interviews with the star performers.

Yet analysing sports television as a complex mix of different genres is useful in understanding the changing tensions that characterise its production and consumption. There has always been a conflict between television's role in purporting to *cover* or *report* sports events and television's role in *promoting* those events by enhancing their entertainment value using the techniques discussed above (Whannel, 1992). Similarly, sports television has always had to reconcile serving the different interests of the already committed sports fan, and the uncommitted 'general viewer', who needs to be won over through promotion. By distinguishing between the different genres that constitute sports television we can evaluate the effects of increasing commodification on the presentation of sport by different broadcasters in different contexts.

A good illustration of this would be a comparison between the coverage of the 2000 Sydney Olympic Games by the BBC and the NBC. Live coverage of nationally and internationally significant sporting competitions such as the Olympics and the men's soccer World Cup is part of the BBC's public service remit, so events were screened live, even though this meant losing the many potential viewers who were asleep or at work during the screening. By contrast, NBC withheld live coverage, preferring instead to provide recorded highlights during prime time in order to generate maximum revenue from advertisers. NBC sought to compensate for the lack of 'liveness' by extensively packaging recorded highlights using video and feature segments that aimed to encourage identification with the personalities and life stories of the star US athletes. As in the 1996 Olympics, NBC identified women as a growth market for this event, and decided to use a stereotypically feminised 'human interest' presentation as part of this strategy (Andrews, 1998).

The significant difference in the way these two broadcasters presented the same visual feed shows how the tensions characterising sports television presentation are resolved in specific national contexts.

Sport and journalism

Spectacular news stories involving sport can easily be recalled: the different types of scandals involving sports celebrities like Ben Johnson, Mike Tyson and Tonya Harding; allegations of greed and corruption surrounding bids to host lucrative events such as the Olympics and the men's soccer World Cup; explicitly jingoistic or xenophobic imagery related to international competitions, for instance in the English tabloid press coverage of the Euro '96 soccer tournament. Examples of the stereotyping of nation, race and gender can often be identified in these spectacular news stories.

The significance of these stories is precisely that they are out of the ordinary. Most journalism concerning sport is much more routine and everyday. There is a danger that in focusing on the most spectacular news related to sport we ignore what sports journalism does day in, day out. This distinction between the spectacular and the routine, I would suggest, corresponds roughly with the two different types of newspaper journalism covering sport. On the one hand, sport features heavily in news in general, most visibly through scandals involving sports personalities. The politics and business of sport are also regular themes within news sections, as is sports-related public disorder when and where it occurs. On the other hand, sports journalism itself is a specialist type of journalism, with professional practices, 'news values' and readerships that are similar to but distinct from those of journalism in general. This section is based on the premise that these two types of journalism cover sport in overlapping but different ways, which occasionally come into conflict – as when sports journalists complain of their relationship of trust with their sources being sabotaged by irresponsible, scandal-chasing news journalists.

In my analysis of sports news I'm going to focus on newspaper journalism. The imbalance between academic studies on newspaper newsrooms and broadcasting newsrooms might represent an implicit recognition that whilst live coverage of sport is obviously the province of broadcasters, the sports news agenda tends to be newspaper-led. This is almost certainly to do with economics. Sport has been seen as economically crucial because it is a means of attracting male readers (particularly younger, affluent ones) to buy a particular newspaper title day after day, and this is reflected in the levels of investment that goes into staffing. The newspaper format assumes that readers want choice between different types of stories, and more investment needs to be given to journalism in order to give this 'breadth of coverage' (Tunstall, 1996: 194). Some of it might also be historical – that newspaper sports journalism was already established by the advent of broadcasting and hence radio and television have always been able to rely on newspapers setting the news agenda. Whether the conclusions around newspaper journalism coverage of sport also hold for television, radio and internet sports journalism would need to be tested.

The key point here is that stories about sports celebrities fit in with scandal stories about celebrities in general, except that the effect is amplified by the contrast between the Apollonian ideal – the role model – and the fallen star. Types of sports-related stories that predominate in the main pages of the newspaper are in general those that fulfil the criteria of newsworthiness as identified by the classic news studies – those news values around personalisation, conflict, etc. I would propose that the news stories found in the rest of the newspaper can be classified into three different types.

The sports scandal. This type of story is the one that predominates in mass circulation and elite publications. The newsworthiness of the story depends on the combination of elements of sex, violence, crime, drugs and greed. Historically, market research surveys have shown that human interest stories appeal simultaneously to different types of readerships in a way that other genres of stories do not (Curran, Douglas and Whannel, 1980; Curran and Sparks, 1991). The scandal story involves a high degree of personalisation, and often focuses on sports stars as celebrities. (In the light of the increasing focus on individuals – even within team games – now promoted by sports marketing organisations, it is reasonable to suggest that there is an increasing number of such stories as the personalities of sports stars achieve ever greater prominence.)

The sports scandal story mainly operates as a sub-genre of the celebrity scandal story. If the celebrity story is important to both broadsheet and tabloid newspapers, those regarding sports celebrities are more so. Rowe (1997) argues that this is because the sports celebrity scandal story represents a case of 'Apollo undone'. The dramatic effect of the hero fallen from grace, a staple of general celebrity narratives, is that much more powerful when the sports star is held up against the Olympic ideal.

Human interest stories, scandal stories, etc. tend to be ignored within news studies in comparison with apparently more important subjects such as war, politics and those which have public policy implications. Human interest stories are treated as ephemeral and marginalised as part of a general dismissal of popular culture as deserving of serious study. This is despite the fact that popular newspapers devote much more of their coverage to such matters, and even elite newspapers at least appear to be carrying more of these types of stories (Curran, Douglas and Whannel, 1980; Curran and Sparks, 1991).

Yet many such stories do foreground important social themes. The studies that have been done on the human interest story tend to focus on their ideological significance: for example, how such stories reproduce normative or stereotypical representations that coincide with dominant ideologies around social class, gender, etc. Sports scandal stories can be seen as particularly important vehicles in this respect, many of them turning, as they do, on normative distinctions: for example, between 'acceptable' and 'unacceptable' violence; between the 'natural' and the 'unnatural'; between 'normal' and 'obsessive' or 'deviant' sexuality and between the acceptable acquisition of wealth and unacceptable forms of corruption. Through such normative distinctions between what is acceptable and what is not, the sports scandal is an ideal vehicle for the representation of negative stereotypes, particularly around 'race', as several stories have shown.

Public policy stories involving sport. These are stories about sport-related matters that have national *public policy* implications, affecting, for example, economic policy (government bids to stage major international competitions); education policy (the role of sport in schools); media policy (cross-ownership between media and sports organisations, the protection of rights to sports events of national significance to ensure universal access); and sports policy itself (how sport can be supported to encourage international success). This type of story tends to be the preserve of broadsheet newspapers, in which public policy has higher news value than it does in the tabloids. If such stories are told at all in popular newspapers, it often tends to be in terms of scandal.

Business news involving sport. Here again, stories involving sport that appear here are those that correspond with the specific news values of the business section. These news values tend to assume a reader who has a professional or financial interest and will treat the news as important information, using it to guide investment decisions (Tunstall, 1996: 354–73). The most common type of stories here involve mergers, takeovers, acquisitions, and possibly also technological developments insofar as they have an effect. The implications of the way in which sport is covered in the business section are obvious: sport is treated as one commodity amongst others.

The production of sports journalism

The introductory paragraph to a recent special issue of the *Columbia Journalism Review* included amongst a number of rhetorical questions: 'Is sports journalism really journalism?' The question astutely summarises concerns raised in this special issue and elsewhere about the professional status of sports journalism (see also Bourgeois, 1995; Garrison and Salwen, 1989, 1994; Rowe and Stevenson, 1995; Salwen and Garrison, 1998). Of particular concern is the blurring of the boundary between sports journalism and sports promotion. This section will address this issue through discussing separately the institutional practices and professional culture, and then the news values of sports journalism.

Sports journalism typically represents the largest specialism within the newspaper, often constituting a separate department with its own editor, desk, sub-editors and reporters. According to Tunstall (1996: 211), in the early 1990s the sports department could often be the most expensive within UK tabloid newspapers. A typical sports department would have a budget of £4m annually and employ sixty journalists, with substantial provision for travel expenses.

As with journalism in general, sports journalism is a product. The requirement to fill a given quotient requires journalists working under pressure to supply copy to deadlines. News production is rationally arranged to achieve this quota through an institutionalisation of routines: a division of labour in the newsroom between editors, sub-editors, reporters and columnists. Typically, reporters will be assigned to particular rounds or beats, which will be their source of daily copy. This system has implications for the kind of news generated, which often originates from press conferences arranged by key organisations on the beat, or from personal relationships with important sources, both on and off the record. Copy tends to be produced from beats, whether or not there is anything to report.

In sports journalism the beat system tends to be organised around particular sports or teams. Lowes has argued (1997, 1999) that the beat system tends to reinforce the bias towards elite, professional sports. Coverage of non-professional sports tends to come in through press releases or information from other news sources. The standardisation of work routines like the beat system also tends to exclude women from sports news (Theberge and Cronk, 1986).

Regarding North American men's sports, there is another element to the beat system that requires a brief discussion. This is to do with access to the players being provided through the locker room pre- and post-game. While access to the locker room is crucial in the US, and provides journalists with quotes that make good copy, at the same time, it also has particular implications. Male sports journalists can feel intimidated by athletes, and are verbally abused and sometimes physically threatened by athletes and their team-mates, aggrieved by what they see as a previous critical report (Plaschke, 2000). This aspect of the locker room environment tends to make journalists think twice about critical coverage. And of course the locker room culture has particular implications for women sports journalists. In the first instance, rights of access to the locker room for women sports journalists had to be won through a sex discrimination lawsuit brought by *Sports Illustrated* writer Melissa Ludtke against the New York Yankees (Creedon, 1994: 87–9). In 1990 the *Boston Herald*'s Lisa Olson was sexually harassed in the New England Patriots locker room (Kane and Disch, 1993). Even when access has been gained, the locker room culture seems specifically designed to make women journalists' jobs difficult (McNamara, 2000).

There tends to be an interdependent relationship between sports organisations and journalists: sports organisations want favourable media coverage, sports journalists want access to sources. This is not to suggest that there are never tensions in this relationship: there are cases where sports organisations have denied access to particular journalists or news organisations, and in these cases journalists have still been able to cover news about sports organisations from other sources. But the normal relationship between sporting organisations and media organisations is one that can be described as mutually beneficial interdependency.

An occasional feature in newspaper sports sections is the 'exclusive' piece, usually an interview with a star, occasionally extracts from an (often ghosted) autobiography, with sports stars, for which newspapers can pay considerable fees. This process is often negotiated through an agent, as part of their diversifying activities. According to Tunstall (1996), the use of such pieces tends to cause professional resentment within competing news organisations at the prospect of stars withholding access from them to take part in such deals. The ownership of exclusive rights by one newspaper does not constrain competing newspapers, as it would in a broadcasting context. Competitors can simply go to other sources, and will often run 'spoilers' on such pieces, often providing more negative stories from available sources.

Sports journalism, however, is not just the product of organised routines and high-pressure deadlines (Rowe, 1999). If we are to understand the production of news content we need also to look at the professional culture of the context in which sports journalists operate: career paths and institutional status, for example. Those working in sports journalism have to deal with a contradiction. On the one hand, sports news is recognised as a means of delivering a large, loyal (mainly young male) readership to advertisers, and is therefore crucial to the economic success of news organisations. Thus those producing it are well rewarded. On the other hand, sports journalism is seen as low prestige, apparently requiring lesser qualifications and being much less challenging than the 'heroic' genres, such as war or political journalism.

This contradiction means that sports journalists tend to stay in their patch: on the one hand, they are well rewarded because of their economic value, on the other hand, their qualities and experience do not tend to be recognised outside the sports department. The personnel of the sports departments of news organisations therefore tends to change less than that of other departments, which has a number of implications. Firstly, it tends to reinforce inequalities: sports journalists are predominantly male, white and middle-class, and because of the lack of mobility in sports journalism, this state of affairs will take time to shift. This, of course, has further implications regarding the ways in which gender and race are represented in media sport. Decisions about whether or how women's sport is represented, and about how women should be targeted as potential audiences are mainly made by men. Similarly, judgements on the achievements and behaviour of black sportsmen and women are predominantly made by white European males. It would be simplistic to assume that this necessarily contributes to negative representations or marginalisation – indeed, it might lead to overcompensation. But what it does mean is that media representations of women and black people are characterised by *difference* – predominantly determined by white men.

There is also the question of prestige within sports news organisations. Some beats confer more prestige and higher salaries than others. These tend to be the beats associated with the elite, male sports, reinforcing the hierarchy of news values within sporting organisations.

This conservative state of affairs might now be changing because of the increasing diversification of the media. The scenario described above may characterise the established media institutions, but workers in the new organisations coming into the media field tend to be more flexible with less room for separate, specialist departments.

The argument of this section is that the production of sports journalism is characterised by relatively fixed organisational structures and a professional culture similar to but distinct from journalism in general. When sports editors and journalists are criticised – for example over the bias towards mens' sport – they will often defend the status quo on the grounds that it is what the readers want.

The news values of sports journalism

It was quarterback Kordell Stewart I was waiting for, a fine young man and a willing if dull interview when he got around to it, but that wasn't what I was thinking. I was thinking: 'How stupid is this? I don't want to wait for this guy. This guy doesn't want me to wait for him. I know what he's going to say. He knows what I'm going to ask. The readers know what I'm going to write. And I know what they're going to say if they read it.' (Collier, 2000: 38)

Here disaffected ex-sportswriter Gene Collier, recalling the moment of revelation when he decided to leave the profession, gives an astute if jaundiced summary of the routine character of sports journalism on an everyday level. One of the dangers of researching and analysing any type of news content is that in focusing on the most spectacular coverage we ignore what journalism does on a routine, everyday basis. In focusing on extraordinary, lurid coverage of sports scandals there is a danger that we can forget that sports journalism is usually very conventional and, to the non-fan, appears banal. Yet this does not mean that the conventions of sports journalism are not significant, indeed they are, because they define the relationship between sports journalism and its readers.

In order to discuss the everyday conventions of sports journalism, I've taken the front page of the sports section of *USA Today* on Monday 9 August 1999 – an unspectacular day in terms of sports news (by which I mean there are no drugs stories, no excessively violent episodes, no action involving athletes currently in the headlines for off-the-field behaviour). The *American Journalism Review* recently claimed of the *USA Today*'s sports section that it had 'come to influence contemporary sports coverage more than any other paper in the country' (Simons, 1999: 72).

The front page carries three reports of the previous day's sporting events: an Oakland Athletics' victory over Chicago White Sox; thoroughbred trainer Elliott Walden's success at the $1m Haskell Invitational race at Oceanport; and Martina Hingis's win over Venus Williams in the TIG classic final. These reports typically begin with a straightforward documentation of the key moments, paying special attention to any statistics that are relevant (something which is reinforced throughout the rest of the sports section). There then follow comments by the participants on the performance.

Below these reports is a 'cover story' headlined 'Vikings aim for redemption. Team enters season focused, but playoff slip-up still stings'. This features the Minnesota Vikings as they prepare for the new season, having the previous season thrown away a 13-point lead to the Atlanta Falcons in the NFC championship game that would have taken them to the Super Bowl. This feature is based on quotes from players about how the team will respond to this failure. Running back Robert Smith is quoted as saying, 'Right now our main focus is Atlanta in the first game, not Atlanta in the last game of last year.' Receiver Cris Carter is quoted in similar vein: 'I don't think the loss is going to drive us. Our desire to be the best is what's going to drive us.' Coach Dennis Green: 'I don't need to look back. Everything I want is ahead of me. I'm not worrying about what happened or who went to the Super Bowl, because it wasn't us.' Minnesota Vikings are reported as putting up a united front when responding to the suggestion that the team will be motivated primarily by the need for revenge in the new season.

I would propose that this is a very typical characteristic of sports journalism: the importance of being 'focused' (Cashmore, 2000, 140–3), of, to use the cliché, 'taking each game as it comes'. Green is reported as keen to distance the Vikings from Denver who, in the words of *USA Today*, 'billed its 1997 season as the Revenge Tour'. What is interesting about this characteristic of sports journalism, is that being focused involves not being affected by the type of 'soap opera emotions' that perhaps elsewhere in the media are used to market sport.

The rest of the article reviews the strengths and weaknesses of the previous year's team through a discussion of statistics, and then discusses player movements and injuries and the effects that these will have on tactics and formation, given the relative strengths of offence and defence, and the balance between veterans and rookies.

This is just a standard, routine piece of sports journalism. What it does is to reinforce the idea that sporting performance can be

distinguished from the rest of social life. The writer discusses anything that might affect the Vikings performance on the pitch: this
includes focus, injuries, player movements, tactics, formation, and
selection. It doesn't include emotions generated from previous
sporting encounters, although this is tested by the newspaper. And
it certainly doesn't include the personal lives of the players. What it
suggests is that managers and players are keen to let fans know,
through the media, that they are unaffected by the soap opera
stuff.

Throughout the *USA Today* sports section there is an emphasis on
statistics, and not just in reports and features. On the front page there
is a USA Snapshots Fact Box: 'a look at statistics that shaped the
sports world'. It features the batting averages of those baseball players who have scored more than 3000 hits. On page 6 a more detailed
graphic details how Wade Boggs and Tony Gwynn scored season by
season since 1982. Pages 4 and 5 provide not just full round-ups,
results and notes from the previous day's American and National
League baseball games, but also a detailed breakdown of full batting,
fielding and pitching averages, using abbreviations with which
readers are assumed to be familiar. These statistics are juxtaposed
with advertisements for fantasy football leagues, indicating the use to
which they might be put.

A common criticism that is made of sports journalism is that this
way of looking at sport – the statistics, the detachment, etc. – is what
makes it 'male'. So how is gender represented throughout the rest of
USA Today? The 'Hingis returns with a vengeance' article is the only
front cover story in which results are related to emotional and physical failings. Hingis returned from a difficult summer, which included
her 'tantrums' at the French Open. Williams explained her 32
unforced errors as due to tiredness. Apart from this and a longer
report on the same tournament inside, there were only two other
reports on women's sport – golf and softball. The article on Hingis is
also noticeable for being written by a female reporter – one of only
two out of twenty bye-lined articles identifiably written by women.
The imbalance between men's and women's sports, and between
male and female contributors, in this particular issue of *USA Today*

supports other research studies into gender and sports journalism (see Chapter 6).

The sports pages feature an almost excessive diet of detailed information about those aspects likely to affect performance, from technical detail in motor sport, to breeding in horse racing. In team sports, player movement, selection, tactics, and any pertinent information likely to have a bearing on an individual player's performance (injuries, attitude, commitment, etc.) are discussed at length. Much sports news functions as a form of gossip. This information can also be of practical use – for example, Fantasy Leagues, and betting (especially spreadbetting as evidenced in the juxtaposition of betting ads with statistics boxes).

News values also determine which types of sport generally tend to be covered (men's rather than women's, professional rather than amateur) and also which particular sports. These hierarchies of news values will be crucial to the later discussion of gender and race.

The audiences for media sport

This chapter has argued that in both the key media discourses through which sport is represented – that is, live coverage and sports journalism – there is a tension between, on the one hand, the use of conventions that have become commonly accepted as means through which events are transparently represented to media audiences and, on the other hand, presentational techniques that are used to increase the value of sport as entertainment. Based on the experience of the last few years, it would be easy to argue that with the development of market-led approaches to presenting and reporting sport, the latter will begin to predominate. On television, the experience of watching an event will become increasingly interactive, with viewers directing their own broadcasts from a variety of different camera positions. However, this ignores the importance of considering the actual context in which audiences and readerships consume sport.

Whereas audience research has become common within media and cultural studies, how viewers and readers consume media sport is a relatively recent and undeveloped subject. Most studies focus on the occasionally problematic behaviour of fans, such as those research projects that test the premise that sports violence increases fans' tendency to become violent in domestic and public situations (for example: Bryant, 1989; Sabo, Gray and Moore, 2000).

Stereotypical images of the television sports fan are widely circulated through a range of popular media – advertisements, sitcoms, dramas, newspaper columns, etc. There is no point in denying that the ritual stereotype of the male sports fan, fuelled by beer and snacks, totally emotionally absorbed in the action as he shouts at the screen, to the almost total exclusion of women, has some basis in experience. This is after all the audience that newspapers want to sell to advertisers. Yet at the same time the stereotype does tend to ignore an important questions: how is the audience constituted for *different* sports and events in terms of the balance between committed sports fans and casual viewers, and/or between men and women?

Gantz and Wenner argue that to understand how the audience consumes media sport, it is important not to conceive of this audience as a 'monolithic mass' (1995: 57). Rather it is important to distinguish between how the audience is constituted between fans and non-fans, or spectators, as each category will react in different ways. They argue that fans are more emotionally involved, more knowledgeable and likely to watch a greater amount of television sport. The balance of categories will also vary in relation to the type of fixture, according to whether it is, for example, a routine sporting event or a special occasion – such as the Olympic Games, or the men's soccer World Cup. The audience for the special occasion will be made up of more non-fans. Fans are most likely to be male – which Gantz and Wenner attribute to sport's role in early child socialisation into gender roles – but they are not exclusively male. In an earlier paper the same researchers propose that 'because many aspects of audience experience with televised sport are distinct from experiences with the rest of television ... further research needs to look beyond social psychological concerns to the subcultures behind fanship of different sports (Wenner and Gantz,1989: 268).

Even allowing that the boundaries between fans and non-fans will not be rigidly drawn, this distinction does help us to think about how media organisations target their audiences. Real and Mechikoff (1992: 323) argue that the 'relationship between the media sports fan and the sporting event closely parallels the position of the ritual participant acting out a mythic celebration'. They draw parallels between media sports and the anthropologist Clifford Geertz's characterisation of the Balinese cockfight as a form of 'deep play' (Geertz, 1973), but argue that the participation of the 'deep fan' is mediated by the media and advertising industries. Eastman and Riggs also argue that the involvement of sports fans with media sporting events often involves complex ritual behaviours (Eastman and Riggs, 1994).

Sport and new media technologies

Finally, no discussion of the changing relationship between media and sport would be complete without some discussion of the role of the internet. From the 'personal' websites that allow sports stars to communicate apparently unmediated to their fans, to the sports news tickers delivering up-to-date play-by-play reports to work desktops, the internet has already provided a variety of new types of service for sports fans. But we should be wary of claims that the internet – in its present personal computer-based form at least – will 'revolutionise' media's relationships with sport. There is always the danger of technological determinism, the idea that new technologies such as the internet will replace old technologies, fundamentally change cultural practices and hence require completely new ways of thinking, without consideration of economic, political, social and cultural contexts through which new technologies are produced and consumed. By contrast, I would propose that in relation to sport, the internet significantly complements existing media technologies but, at least for the foreseeable future, may affect but will not supplant television, radio and newspapers' role in mediating sport. There are considerable continuities between the production, content and consumption of sport via the old technologies and via the internet. At the same time the internet holds promise in researching and analysing the relationship between mediated sport and its fans, even if this means a modification of established ways of thinking about this relationship rather than a fundamental transformation.

There are two aspects of sport on the internet that I want to focus on here. The first is the role of the internet in the *commodification* of sport. At the time of writing this book, early business optimism in the profitability of 'dot.com' companies was replaced by concern that start-up and running costs were not being matched by revenues, concern that was manifest in falling share values and some spectacular failures. But whereas a number of household names on the internet are only expected to be profitable in the long term, internet companies producing sports content are already generating significant revenue. To suggest why sport works financially where other internet businesses sometimes don't, we can draw on what we have already discussed about the relationship between media sport and fans.

As indicated by the section on the news values of sports journalism, committed sports fans are hungry for particular types of content: up-to-the-minute news that is likely to have an effect on team's performance (injuries, player movements, etc.), statistics, fixtures and reports – substantially the same type of content as provided by newspapers such as *USA Today* (see pp. 41–3) but even more up-to-the-minute. Indeed, many sports news sites are actually run by established sports news organisations, alongside emerging independent ones. These sites are able to attract the same type of audiences for advertisers as newspapers – the predominantly young male readership fits well with the demographic character of internet users. Further, if the resources of the content provider allow, the internet is able to offer relevant information to geographically displaced fans of less newsworthy teams – making it possible for fans to keep informed about team news in distant parts of the country, or even in a different country. Such information was previously only available to consumers of newspapers and/or broadcasting services *in that area*. With respect to sports fandom, the internet transforms the significance of place, not eradicating it, but if anything strengthening individual loyalties.

By contrast, the internet provides a space for communication between fans through website chat rooms and bulletin boards, and through newsgroups. These provide a form of expression for fans that can also function as a research tool. For example, referring back to the *USA Today* article on the Minnesota Vikings, there is a very active newsgroup, alt.sports.football.mn-vikings, through which fans discuss plays, selections, individual players' performances, motivation and abilities. The concerns of contributors to the newsgroups are broadly consistent with those of sports journalism.

We need to be cautious, however, about the extent to which fans who use the internet or newsgroups are likely to be representative of fans as a whole. Economic factors such as the varying costs of online time and hardware, and the cultural differences associated with different sports, will affect the level of participation in these groups. For example, while there are heavy postings to the newsgroups of most of the North American major league teams, there are far fewer newsgroups dedicated to English soccer teams. This difference reflects differences between the US and UK in access to the internet, and cannot be taken to show that the traditional culture of soccer fandom prizes attendance at games over mediated experience.

Scare stories in the UK media have focused on the use of the internet by soccer hooligans to organise fights. Here again, care needs to be exercised in treating any such postings unproblematically. Under conditions of anonymity, anyone can assume the identity of a soccer hooligan, or any other identity.

These qualifications do not invalidate the research and analysis of sports fans' expression on the internet – but we should be careful not to treat these as a simple reflection of fans views, but rather as itself a *mediated* form.

Sport on the internet tends to supplement provision for the committed sports fan; the casual viewer is unlikely to make much use of the facility. The nature of the technology – with the computer being predominantly 'sit-up' rather than 'sit-back' – and the importance of interactivity and hyperlinking – ideally suited to the needs of the sports fan who actively seeks information or wants to participate in discussion – may mean that the voice of the general viewer is underrepresented.

There is another type of provision that the internet can provide –
live, streaming video of sporting events. Setting aside the severe technical limitations of this format, which restrict its effective use to
those connected to advanced broadband networks, once again, it is
important to consider the often collective context in which media
sport is consumed. It is unlikely that sitting up to watch the usually
smaller monitor screens will replace watching sport on television.
The value of live streaming video is likely to be where it can be used
to fill gaps left by broadcasting. At the 2000 Sydney Olympics, the
International Olympic Committee took legal action to close websites
whose footage, it was feared, would contravene NBC's agreement
with advertisers to delay as-live coverage until US prime-time
(Dodson and Barkham, 2000).

|3|

The globalisation and commodification of sport

Anecdotal evidence of the global character of sport can be found reported in the media on a daily basis. To take some random illustrations from 1999: Manchester United launched a new away kit simultaneously in Manchester and Kowloon, where they were in the middle of a lucrative pre-season tour of China, Hong Kong and Australia; Welsh team coach Graham Henry – himself a New Zealander – included Australian-born and bred Jason Jones Hughes in his Rugby World Cup squad on the basis of the player's Welsh father; the Malaysian Grand Prix was run for the first time as part of FIA boss Bernie Ecclestone's strategy to stage more races outside Europe, partly due to the European Union's tobacco advertising bans; and Michael Jordan retired, a basketball player whose global celebrity status made him known even in nations where NBA basketball was not transmitted.

These cases, which could easily be exchanged for others, indicate how fundamental and complex is the globalisation of sport. Sporting events are now regularly transmitted live to spectators on the opposite side of the world. Images of sports stars are reproduced and circulated internationally not just by television and the press but also via the Internet, advertising and feature films. And star performers are now able to seek employment on a global basis. The idea of globalisation – that the world is increasingly characterised by processes that transcend the boundaries of the nation – has become commonplace in the discussion of current issues in sport. This chapter looks at the concept of globalisation in detail, and argues that it is extremely useful in understanding what is going on in the world of sport. Conversely, sport provides an excellent example of how globalisation needs to be understood as a complex set of economic, political and cultural processes.

Conflicting definitions of globalisation

Globalisation is not a universally accepted concept. Even amongst those who argue that it fundamentally affects everyday life, there are many varied perspectives on what aspects of globalisation are important, and therefore what implications follow. Globalisation has become a major issue in many academic disciplines, particularly in economics, politics and sociology, as well as in interdisciplinary subjects such as media and cultural studies. Inevitably, each tends to prioritise aspects of globalisation that reflect the discipline's own concerns, whether economic, political, social or cultural.

Held *et al.* (1999) provide a useful framework for understanding different perspectives on globalisation by identifying three different perspectives, which they summarise as those held by 'hyperglobalisers', sceptics and 'transformationalists'.

> For the *hyperglobalisers* ... contemporary globalisation defines a new era in which peoples everywhere are increasingly subject to the disciplines of the global marketplace. By contrast the *sceptics* ... argue that globalisation is essentially a myth which conceals the reality of an international economy increasingly segmented into three major regional blocs in which national governments remain very powerful. Finally, for the *transformationalists* ... contemporary patterns of globalisation are conceived as historically unprecedented such that state and societies across the globe are experiencing a process of profound change as they try to adapt to a more interconnected but highly uncertain world. (Held *et al.*, 1999: 2)

How would recent global tendencies in sport be interpreted according to these perspectives?

To take 'hyperglobalisation' first. Held *et al.* (1999) cite the work of business writer Kenichi Ohmae as typical of the hyperglobalisation argument. In his influential book *Borderless World* (1990) Ohmae asserts that we are moving into an unprecedented phase of globalisation that effectively makes national borders irrelevant. If this perspective is to be applied to sport, globalisation is an inevitable and irresistible process in which sports participants, administrators and fans are subject to the forces of a global economy operating beyond the regulatory reach of nation-states. In this scenario, capital and resources would flow to those places in the world which are comparatively deregulated, whereas those where national regulation is used to protect vulnerable values associated with sport risk losing out on the revenue needed to build successful facilities, teams and athletes. Political intervention at a national, regional or local level can play a subsidiary role – such as when nations compete with each other for the prestige and profit of staging the major global sports events, and national governments work with national sporting bodies to provide training and facilities for young athletes. Taken to extremes, in a 'borderless world', even the idea of national teams based on qualification requirements of either birth or parental lineage could be seen as representing restraint of trade.

The argument that sport has to adapt to the demands of the global economy is one regularly heard from transnational media and sport companies and profitable sports clubs, as well as from market-led reformers amongst politicians and sports administrators.

By contrast, a 'sceptical' perspective on global sport would see the above definition of globalisation as a myth that justifies the national re-regulation of media and sport to suit the financial interests of transnational media corporations and profitable sports clubs. Further, these economic developments are not truly 'global' but organised around regional blocs: Europe, the Americas and East Asia/Pacific Rim. Held *et al.* (1999) cite Hirst and Thompson's *Globalisation in Question* (1996) as exemplifying this approach – a book which uses quantitative analysis to refute the argument that the international economy is now more 'globalised'.

Resistance to the inevitable globalisation of sport as a myth can be found expressed through the statements of representatives of sports fans' organisations, journalists, national administrators, national and local politicians. The takeover of the globally popular English soccer club Manchester United by Rupert Murdoch's BSkyB in 1998-99 was blocked by the UK Labour government following a campaign organised by a broad coalition involving the Independent Manchester United Supporters' Association, Shareholders United Against Murdoch, the fans' organisations of other English clubs, the national Football Supporters' Association, the *Daily Mirror* and other national newspapers also not owned by Murdoch, and sympathetic journalists and politicians (Brown and Walsh, 1999).

These perspectives may be poles apart on the issue of whether globalisation exists, and on its implications. However, what they have in common is that they treat the issue of globalisation as predominantly economic. By contrast, I argue that the significance of the globalisation of sport cannot be explained purely in terms of economics. While the role of television and sponsorship in the process of commodification is central and will be discussed in detail below, what is crucial to understanding the globalisation of sport is its cultural significance.

Here Held *et al.*'s third, 'transformational', perspective is useful. This has been described by Giddens (1990: 64) as:

> The intensification of worldwide social relations which link distant localities in such a way that local happenings are shaped by events occurring many miles away and vice versa. This is a dialectical process because such local happenings may move in an obverse direction from the very distanciated relations that shape them. Local transformation is as much a part of globalisation as the lateral extension of social connections across time and space.

According to this perspective, local events are not subject to the laws of a distant, omnipotent global economy. Rather there is a dialectical and dynamic relationship between, on the one hand, global economic and political forces shaped by transnational companies and organising bodies, and, on the other hand, national and local actors operating within specific local and national contexts (e.g. politicians, fans). The outcomes of these conflicts is uncertain and not guaranteed in advance. And further analysis of the effects of global economic and political developments in media sport (as well as national and local policy responses to these developments) requires attention to the different types of contexts in which these forces operate, paying particular attention to the cultural significance of media sport and the ways in which it functions as part of lived experience.

This chapter argues that while there is nothing *inevitable* about globalisation, at the same time the processes it describes have had fundamental effects on sport. Transnational capitalism might have played a major role in these processes, but in pursuit of their interests they may well encounter local and national resistance. And more particularly, while the media and communications industries may be implicated in sport globalisation they also can provide space for the expression of national and local opposition. In other words, if the concept of globalisation is to be useful it needs to be understood in all of its complexity.

I shall follow a commonly accepted practice of discussing the different *economic*, *political* and *cultural* aspects of the globalisation of sport (see, for example, Waters, 1995). However, whereas such a distinction might be analytically useful, it will quickly become apparent that the economic, political and the cultural are inextricably interlinked and difficult to separate in practice (Donnelly, 1996).

The 'post-industrialisation' of sport

In order to understand the economic and cultural implications of recent developments in the globalisation of sport, I propose that these changes should be seen as forming part of a wider economic transformation commonly identified as post-industrialisation or post-Fordism, in which sport is increasingly subject to commodification (see for example Andrews, 1997; Cole and Hribar, 1995). Many sports historians have argued that commercialisation was prevalent during the nineteenth century (for example, see Polley, 1998). Indeed, as Whitson (1998: 58) suggests, as soon as sport was professionalised, this immediately returned 'to ordinary people, as paying spectators, commodified versions of practices with which they had once entertained themselves'. Yet in accepting that elements of commercialisation can be traced right back to the origins of modern sport, we should not underestimate the fundamental impact of the changes over the last two decades or so of the twentieth century.

The worldwide sports industry now constitutes 3 per cent of world trade, according to one estimate (Koranteng, 1998: 3). And television has been central to this expansion, not just through the sale of the rights to cover events but also through one of the key activities within this industry – the global marketing of sports events and personalities. Further, over the last twenty years or so, the economic structure of television sport has undergone a fundamental transformation in line with the general move from an industrial to a post-industrial, or post-Fordist economy.

The economic importance of centralised, rationalised, standardised industrial production for mass markets based on economies-in-scale (spreading fixed costs over high production runs) has been complemented by a more decentralised global economy based on specialised production ('contracting out', often on a global scale) and segmented markets. The industrial model is based on the production of material goods; the post-industrial model is more concerned with image – the economy of 'sign and space', as Lash and Urry put it (1994).

The sportswear company Nike has become the paradigm example of this newer form of global, flexible model of production. Nike's design and marketing is based at its headquarters in the USA, but its production is contracted out to South-East Asia. The value of Nike's products is related to their design rather than their use-value. Nike's marketing is based on a range of differentiated products. For example, Nike training shoes are priced across a wide range, but the added value of the higher-priced shoes is to do with scarcity, celebrity

endorsement and design rather than the cost of materials and production. Nike is typical of the post-industrial economy dependent on
image – not just the cultural and social meanings of commodities but
also more elusive and intangible aspects such as design and style
(Goldman and Papson, 1998; see also Harvey, Rail and Thibault,
1996). As Cole and Hribar note: 'Phil Knight [Nike's chief executive]
and the sneaker are to post-Fordism what Henry Ford and the car
were to Fordism' (1995: 363).

It could be argued that from the 1940s to the 1970s sports television was produced according to an industrial model. From the
launch of radio in the 1920s, broadcasting has been characterised by
the distinction between the public service model followed by
European broadcasters and the commercial model followed by US
broadcasters. In the UK, techniques of television sport presentation
were developed through the institution of the BBC (Whannel, 1992).
Broadcasters negotiated directly with sports organisations, and the
key issue facing sports administrators was not the costs of television
rights but whether or not televised coverage would reduce event
attendances. Television sport presentation was the responsibility of
an outside broadcast unit that was a department of the BBC, and was
also responsible for covering other live events. The launch of the
commercial ITV network in 1955 did not make as much difference as
might have been expected. ITV was regulated according to a public
service model, and BBC and ITV effectively constituted a duopoly.
Although the US networks – ABC, CBS and NBC – were commercial,
they effectively comprised an oligopoly (Bellamy, 1998). There are
fundamental differences between the ways in which European and
US broadcasting has been regulated with regard to the balance
between commercial and public service imperatives. However in
both Europe and Western Europe, broadcasters operated effectively
in monopoly, duopoly or oligopoly conditions, able to keep the costs
of sports rights relatively low and to sustain high production because
of the lack of competitors.

The transition to a post-industrial or post-Fordist economy
should be seen as the product of a complex range of economic,
technological and political developments. New technologies, partic-

ularly information technologies, have been central to the transition from an industrial to a post-industrial economy. And new technologies are fundamental to television sport. The impact of satellite technology, starting with the Tokyo Olympics in 1964, is often assessed according to its ability to simultaneously transmit live pictures of global sporting events around the world. But in many ways the impact of technology on sports television is as much to do with the emergence of new distributive technologies: cable and direct broadcast satellite. The enhanced capacity offered by cable and satellite delivery systems was crucial to the launch of specialist sports channels such as ESPN and Sky Sports. Encryption has enabled broadcasters to offer pay-TV and pay-per-view services. Digitalisation will allow further increased capacity, leading to the possibility of more specialised sports channels and greater interactivity. Technology has also improved market intelligence through improved ratings-gathering methods, and cable and digital systems offer detailed ratings information immediately. To sum up, the main impact of technological development is that it has enabled the shift towards market segmentation.

Apart from new technologies, the other crucial factor in the transition from industrial to post-industrial media sport has been the global market-led re-regulation of the media. This re-regulation has been enacted at the level of national governments in response to transnational political institutions and summits (the World Trade Organisation and the European Union are just two transnational political organisations whose decisions have a bearing on the environment in which global media sport companies operate). Briefly, national governments have tended to deregulate to remove 'public interest' clauses, national content restrictions and quotas, and media ownership restrictions, and to re-regulate to encourage privatisation. This has had a major effect in Europe, which traditionally has been public service, but it has also had an effect even in the more 'lightly regulated' USA, where the removal of restrictions on the ownership of television networks by film studios, enabled Disney's takeover of ABC/Capital Cities in 1995, which included acquisition of the ESPN and the ESPN2 networks.

From around 1980 a more 'post-industrial' model began to emerge. The driving force behind this was the emergence of new competitors benefiting either from political re-regulation and/or technological innovation. In the UK Channel 4 was launched in 1982, a channel which commissioned its original programming entirely from independent production companies. The independent company Cheerleader became known for more exciting presentational techniques, innovative in terms of British sports television, and its coverage of previously under-represented sports (Maguire, 1990, 1993a; Holland, 1997). And the key development in television sport in the UK was the launch of the satellite channel Sky Sports in competition with British Satellite Broadcasting (BSB) in 1989. These channels merged to form BSkyB. The new channels adopted a dual strategy of acquiring exclusive television rights to premier events, and screening pre-packaged magazine programmes at low cost. The emergence of BSkyB broke the informal BBC and ITV cartel, which operated to keep costs down.

In the United States the industrial model was affected by the breaking of the big three oligopoly by a combination of technological developments and political re-regulation in the interests of the market. As a result, the Fox network of local cable stations emerged in the 1980s, with the launch of specialist cable channels such as ESPN and the regional sports networks (Bellamy, 1998).

The re-regulation of television in the UK has led to a more complex and competitive environment in which independent production has expanded due to its lower costs. This shift has been described as a move from the 'factory' model of television sport production to the 'publisher' and 'packager' models (Tunstall, 1993: 68):

> The publisher model became much commoner, as both BBC and ITV (as well as Channel Four) contracted out the coverage of some entire sports to independent production companies. In addition, the packager model was pursued by BSkyB as it specialized on providing an endless flow of live sport, mainly acquired en masse from Europe and the USA.

In this situation, heads of television sports departments are now more involved in financial planning and in negotiating with a range of parties for television rights. They negotiate increasingly with agents representing sports associations. So an industrial model of television sports production, dominated by monolithic institutions such as the US networks and the European public service broadcasting organisations, has given way to a more competitive 'post-industrial' model in which established broadcasters have had to modernise themselves to compete in a more 'flexible' context.

This transition in the production and consumption of television sport is inextricably related to the emergence alongside broadcasters and sports bodies of a third sector, which could be described as sports marketing and management companies. These companies pursue a wide range of activities, including those previously associated with either broadcasting or sports organisations. They buy and sell television rights, and are involved in management, marketing, consultancy, programme production, internet services, and team ownership, blurring the boundaries between the different activities carried out by media and sports organisations. Hence the notion of a global media–sport production complex becomes increasingly relevant.

A sign of the rapid change affecting media sport was the inauguration in 1990 of Sportel, the International Sports and Television Convention held each Autumn in Monaco, effectively the sports equivalent of the media trade fair MIPCOM in Cannes, which brings together television companies, programme sales companies, sports organisers, events promoters and sponsors. The convention was embraced by the creation of the General Association of International Sports Federations (GAISF), which also has an official magazine, *SportVision*, in which most of the major media and sports management companies take full page advertising. An American version (SportelAmerica) has been run each spring from 1997 (Serafini: 2000).

The media sport sector epitomises developments in the modern entertainment industry as a whole in its emphasis on *licensing* and *talent*. In his insightful analysis of the economics of the cultural industries, Frith (1996: 166) argues that

the most significant source of income in the entertainment
industry ... is *not* the manufacture and exchange of goods to
individual customers for cash ... but the fee income from *licensing* the rights to various *uses* of the property.

This provides a good summary of what is happening in the economics of media sport. Television sports rights are viewed as *properties* to
be licensed over and over again, in different formats and in different
markets. Typically, television rights to a sporting event can be
licensed once for the whole event live; again for the edited highlights
shortly after, and later for a variety of other packages of recorded
sport. Additionally, television rights are licensed in different regions
of the world. For example, it is well known that the partnership
between the English Premier League and BSkyB since 1992 has had a
ground-breaking effect on the media sports environment in the UK,
but in 1997 the Premier League sold TransWorldInternational and
Canal Plus the overseas rights for $170m. (Koranteng, 1998: 27).
Rights can be exploited every time footage of a sports event is shown:
from weekly sports review programmes such as TWI's TransWorld
Sport, right through to 'bloopers' programmes. Conversely, the
licensing of permission to broadcast events also requires restrictions
on unlicensed coverage – short clips are exempt from licensing for
use in news programmes, and even then the length of the clip is limited and the rightholders' logo indicated.

The escalating costs of rights have encouraged tendencies towards
convergence of ownership – a worldwide trend in the media sector.
Sports media and management companies will typically offer a range
of services: ESPN International owns the rights to a whole range of
events, including North American events (NFL, NHL) and Brazilian
soccer, but also owns the Cayton library. Rights holders such as
International Sport and Leisure further maximise revenue from these
rights by making official films and television programmes themselves.

And, just as in the entertainment industry as a whole, hand-in-
hand with the increased emphasis on the licensing of rights goes
the ownership of *talent*. The star industry is as important in sports
as it is in popular music or film. Stars increasingly earn their

income not just through team salaries and bonuses, or through prize money and appearance fees, but through brand endorsement. In August 1999 Nike announced unprecedented sponsorship deal with Tiger Woods (Davies, 1999). This more complicated set of arrangements has also contributed to the rise in the number of sports agents representing athletes, teams and sponsors in their negotiation, again contributing to the growth of the marketing and management sector between broadcasters and sports organisers. The star industry in major sports has led to very visible conflicts whereby sports stars, believing that their value to their team is greater than their salary, have withheld their labour in one way or another. The most famous recent example was in 1994 and 1995 when MLB was crippled by a players' strike initiated by the attempt to impose a salary cap. In Europe in 1998 and 1999 there was the spectacle of a number of soccer players seeking transfers to more lucrative contracts, submitting doctors' notes claiming stress as a reason for not turning up for work.

And just as the increasing economic importance of rights leads to the blurring of boundaries between the activities of different types of organisations, broadcasters and sports management companies also seek to own sports talent directly through the acquisition of profitable sports teams. The most globally visible owner is News Corporation, which owns the LA Dodgers and has interests in the New York Knicks (basketball) and New York Rangers (hockey). But other companies own sports teams as well. Disney bought the Anaheim Mighty Ducks after films of the same name. Since the merger of Disney with ABC/Capital Cities, the Mighty Ducks can now be seen on ESPN. In the UK broadcasters have been discouraged from bidding for sports team ownership by the UK government's block of the takeover of Manchester United, but Carlton and NTL have shown interest in Arsenal and Newcastle United, respectively. In France, Canal Plus own Paris St Germain and in Italy, Fininvest own A.C. Milan.

There are several advantages to the vertical integration of sports and media. Firstly there is cross-promotion: media outlets can be used to promote sports teams. Thus News Corporation's newspapers welcomed BSkyB's bid for Manchester United in 1998: on the day the bid launched Murdoch's *Sun* welcomed it with the headline 'Gold Trafford'. One of the problems for media companies is that in promoting a competition they also inflate the price the administrative body will charge them next time. This is the case with BSKy B and the Premier League. At least media companies' ownership of teams allows some of that money to come back. However, if negotiation of rights is a matter for the clubs (as in Italy and Spain), then media companies can obtain full benefit of building the brand through not having to subsequently pay rights fees inflated by the activities of the media company itself.

The direct ownership of clubs by broadcasters and other companies may well put an end to the kind of arrangements whereby sports competitions and leagues negotiate collectively on behalf of clubs and spread revenues equitably for the good of the competitions as a whole. Already Spanish and Italian soccer clubs negotiate directly with broadcasters or other companies, and do so either individually or in groups. In June 1999, Barcelona tied up a five-year deal, from 2003, with pay-per-view operator Vía Digital worth £250m (*Observer* 13 June 1999). In the UK the making of collective arrangements has been challenged as a cartel in the courts by the Office of Fair Trading, in the name of consumer protection. Although the case was thrown out, deregulatory pressures may well win in the long term.

Central to the transformations of the media-sport industry is that many of the new players in the market operate transnationally. Indeed, the ability of either sports organisations or media companies to commercially exploit a sport depends on its potential for transnational sales. Even US major league sports now recognise the need to sell overseas, despite the historical advantage of the size of their home market. So the potential for expansion of those sports that are only played or watched in a small number of nations, such as Rugby League, is limited.

There is a very small number of companies who attempt a genuinely worldwide presence. News Corporation has the Fox network in the US, Sky Latin America, BSkyB, and Star in South-East Asia.

ESPN has two networks in the US (ESPN2 and ESPNews). ESPN International has three networks covering specific footprints: ESPN Latin American, ESPN 'Asia and the Pacific Rim', and ESPN 'Middle East/North Africa', as well as interests in Eurosport, Sky and the Japan Sports Channel (Bellamy, 1998: 77). ESPN also has interests in Eurosport. ESPN itself is owned by ABC/Capital Cities/Disney. However, as this brief discussion has shown, the transnational marketing strategies adopted by such media companies are based on a division of the world into regional footprints based on industry perceptions of market viability. None of these companies show much interest in sub-Saharan Africa, for example. As Sreberny-Mohammadi (2000) notes in her discussion of global communications, media globalisation tend to extend mainly to those parts of the world which are seen to sustain lucrative markets.

Major transformations in the economic structures of media sport are often brought about by the emergence of transnational companies seeking to break up established national arrangements. The most aggressive of these companies has been Murdoch's News Corporation. In the US the Fox network has had a fundamental effect on media sport since its launch in 1986. Fox has used sport to challenge ABC, NBC and CBS, through bankrolling expensive television rights deals at a time when the existing networks were expressing concerns about escalating costs. Fox acquired television rights for the NFL from 1993. In the UK BSkyB acquired the domestic rights to the new soccer Premier League from 1992. In both cases News Corporation used sport to challenge existing duopolistic or oligopolistic arrangements.

This has transformed national broadcasting. Even public service broadcasters have had to compete with transnational companies for sports rights and markets on a global basis, often involving partnership with commercial companies. European 'listed events' legislation in some countries prevents cable and satellite broadcasters from showing global events such as the men's soccer World Cup and the Olympic Games on an exclusive basis, but such legislation cannot guarantee that national terrestrial broadcasters will actually be able to acquire the rights themselves. The established broadcasters are finding difficulty covering the spiralling costs of sports rights. The BBC has recently lost key rights because of competing demands for its funding. The US networks, even the newcomer Fox, have a different problem – tensions with local affiliates who carry a mix of network and local programming over the share-out of diminishing advertising revenue in the context of the emergence of new media ('Networks stare death in face', *Observer Business*, 6 June 1999).

And inextricably related to all these shifts is sponsorship. Once again, sponsorship is not new. Examples of sponsorship of sports teams and events can be traced in the nineteenth century, and today's sponsors have been sponsoring events from the 1920s. What has changed is the level of coordination of sponsorship, for which the sports marketing companies have been largely responsible.

Sponsorship is seen by sports marketing companies as particularly effective. The use of logos on sportswear and advertising is seen as a marketing strategy which is unintrusive but at the same time leads to increased brand recognition compared to other forms of advertising. 'Circuits of promotion' are established when a company buys exclusive rights to the use of a trademark (Whitson, 1998). The sponsor purchases the right to use the Olympic symbol because of all the associations that go with that symbol. Then through the use of its advertising, those associations are confirmed, leading to a mutual amplification of the value of the event and of the company.

Television sport producers are operating in a highly competitive environment. The economics for commercial broadcasters seem at first sight to be simple. Revenue is generated from advertising and sponsorship, or a combination of this with income from pay-TV. Expenditure includes television rights and the costs of production. However, for commercial channels sports television can be used as a vehicle for self-promotion, as the ability to carry nationally important sporting events confers prestige on a channel. This is particularly significant for public service broadcasters, as is demonstrated when the broadcaster loses the rights to national events – the loss of rights to test match cricket was represented as a disaster for the BBC. Yet even public service broadcasters are subject to the demands of the marketplace. Political pressure to keep costs down combined with a restriction on public finance at a time of sports rights inflation has led the BBC into the same commercial world as other broadcasters: using independent producers, national public service broadcasters are forced to compete with transnational corporations in order to retain the ability to transmit events in their home countries, despite any domestic regulations intended to keep major events available to all.

This section has argued that since the 1980s the media sport industry has been subject to the *intensification* of the processes of globalisation and commodification, even whilst recognising that these processes have always characterised organised sport. These changes should be understood as part of a shift towards a post-industrial global economy, in which the economic value of both media and sport as part of the cultural industries is recognised as increasingly important. Although examples of where sport has played a major role in introducing new television services can easily be found, the influence of media economics on sport has been predominant.

Unsurprisingly, the same tendencies that have affected the global media industry in general – towards concentration and convergence of ownership, towards vertical and horizontal integration, and towards placing ever greater value on rights and talent – also characterise media sport. Further, sport plays a central role within the transnational strategies adopted by many media corporations – yet these are transnational strategies that prioritise particular markets and exclude others.

The global politics of FIFA and the IOC

One of the main themes of debates on globalisation is the extent to which political power is being transferred from nation-states to transnational organisations, such as the European Union and the World Trade Organisation. Both these organisations have affected the context in which sport operates. For example, the Bosman ruling at the European Court of Justice in December 1995 cited an Article of the Treaty of Rome intended to remove barriers to freedom of labour within the European Union's boundaries (Giulianotti, 1999:

121–2). This legal judgement has quickened the spiral of higher top player salaries and consequently higher price of rights in European soccer. The WTO, which has been set up to enforce the terms of the GATT (General Agreement on Tariffs and Trade), promotes unrestricted trade worldwide, and endorses retaliatory action against nations which are perceived to be following protectionist policies. Media and sport have not yet been major issues – although French film was a stumbling block at the Uruguay Round of negotiations of the GATT. Nevertheless the GATT and the WTO have encouraged a deregulatory climate towards media regulation, within which governments have abolished or weakened foreign ownership restrictions, national content quotas, public service requirements and production subsidies, leading to a more competitive broadcasting environment. Further moves in this direction can be expected from both quarters. The European Union's drive towards political harmonisation and free competition might pose more problems for national leagues and competitions negotiating television rights collectively, such as the UK's soccer Premier League, given that in other European nations teams negotiate television rights individually. And as the economic importance of the media and sport industries are increasingly recognised, any national regulation that can be perceived as protectionist, for example, 'listed events' regulation, may well come under further scrutiny.

However, in discussing the role of political institutions as agents of the globalisation of sport, analysis of its own international administrative bodies is crucial. The Federation Internationale de Football Association (FIFA), the governing body of world soccer, and the International Olympic Committee (IOC) are the most important of these organisations. Formed respectively in 1907 and 1895, both predate by some years many of those political institutions more commonly identified as the main political agents of globalisation. And they now generate significant revenue through television rights and sponsorship, which rivals the gross national product of many nation-states. FIFA has been estimated to be worth $250 billion dollars a year (Sugden and Tomlinson, 1998: 1). Since the mid-1980s both organisations have been responsible for major political decisions which have important economic consequences – particularly in the selection of host venues for their respective major events which can confer significant economic benefits on the successful city or nation.

There is a substantial literature on FIFA and the IOC, and there is little space here to do justice to a proper summary of this work (see Hill, 1993, and Sugden and Tomlinson, 1998, as valuable introductions to the respective organisations). Instead this section seeks to provide a brief comparative analysis of the role of these institutions as agents of globalisation.

Both bodies were formed within a decade of each other. The International Olympic Committee was formed in 1895 to organise the first modern Olympics the next year. FIFA was formed in 1904 by seven European nations, although its first major competition, the men's soccer World Cup, did not follow until 1930. The inauguration of both organisations came during the take-off period for the globalisation of sport, between 1870 and 1930, a period during which many existing international contests and administrative bodies came into existence (Horne, Tomlinson and Whannel, 1999). This take-off period of the globalisation of sport can be seen to parallel the more general intensification of globalisation (see, for example, Robertson 1990). The international governance of sport is inseparable from global politics on a wider scale, with imbalances/inequalities in representation mirroring broader economic and political relations. Early in their existence the IOC and FIFA were dominated by European countries, and the more recent story of the organisations has been about the extent to which European countries have prepared to, or been made to, relinquish power, firstly under threat from South America, and, later, from Africa. Such shifts are inextricable from the broader process of decolonisation, with newly independent nations applying for membership to these organisations as part of the process of nation-building.

The universalist and internationalist ideals of both organisations contrasts with the internal political conflicts that have characterised their histories. The histories of both reveal a Eurocentric bias. De Coubertin's original invitations to participate in the 1896 Olympics were sent out to sports organisations in Europe, the USA and

Australia. FIFA's initial membership consisted of seven European nations. The limited number of presidents that both organisations have had over a century have accentuated the Eurocentric bias. By 2001, six of the seven IOC presidents have all held European nationalities, the other being an American, and all but one notable exception of the eight FIFA presidents have been European.

The second half of the twentieth century has seen a more complex picture emerge, in which FIFA and the IOC can no longer be seen as simply instruments of European imperialism. According to Sugden and Tomlinson, FIFA '*also* articulates the interests of the Third World' (1998: 224) – a conclusion that can also be generally applied to the IOC. FIFA and the IOC have provided the arena for the expression of 'Third World' interests paralleling similar developments in non-governmental organisations such as the UN and UNESCO (ibid: 225).

The economic transformation of both organisations has been supervised by two charismatic presidents – Juan Antonio Samaranch, IOC President 1980-2001; and Joao Havelange, FIFA president 1974–97 – who share the policy of funding global expansionism through aggressive commercial exploitation. To be elected, both appealed to 'third world' concerns over European domination. Havelange was a successful businessman – in contrast to figures such as Stanley Rous, who treated the job as 'public service'. However, the politics of funding global expansion through increased commercialisation is fraught with contradiction.

Further, both organisations have been characterised by potential conflicts of interest between their constituent bodies. FIFA has six powerful confederations that tend to polarise into a conflict between the European body, UEFA, representing the richest, historically privileged group, and the other confederations: CONMEBOL (South America), CONCACAF (North and Central America), CAF (Africa), AFC (Asia) and OFC (Oceania). A particularly contentious issue between these six confederations has been the allocation of World Cup places. Europe has always been over-represented in proportion to the number of its members. In the 1998 World Cup Europe claimed 47 per cent of the places, though its member countries constitute 26 per cent of total FIFA membership. This conflict was exemplified by the AFC walkout from a FIFA meeting over the reduction of the number of qualifying places (from 4 to 3) allocated to Asia and Oceania in the 2002 World Cup, due to Japan and Korea both being automatically represented as joint hosts. This Eurocentric bias has long been recognised and since 1974 the number of places allocated to the confederations outside Europe and South America has increased. However, this expansion has been achieved through increasing the number of participating nations in the finals so that neither UEFA or CONMEBOL have to sustain a cut in their real allocation. The commodification of the game has only served to reinforce this bias: Europe and South America represent the biggest and most lucrative television markets for soccer.

The internal politics of the IOC are characterised not just by organisations representing national interests (the National Olympic Committees) but also by international federations representing particular sports. Here, distribution of revenues, predominantly generated by television revenues and sponsorship, is a contentious issue. Organisations aim to obtain a share of television rights revenue which reflects their ability to bring in the audience. The US Olympic Committee gets a guaranteed proportion of television money on the basis that it brings in the majority of the audience. And the powerful IAAF (International Amateur Athletics Federation), headed by Primo Nebiolo, its president from 1981 until his death in 1999, has argued for a greater share of revenue on the grounds that athletics is usually the most watched part of the Olympic Games.

The recent history of the IOC and FIFA is inextricable from the post-industrialisation of sport discussed in the section above. Both the IOC and FIFA have not just benefited from the increasing revenue derived from television rights and sponsorship that have characterised the period, they have also been principal agents in contributing to these processes.

Both bodies have used a massive increase in the revenue generated by television rights and sponsorship to fund expansion. In 1960, the cost of US television rights to the Rome Olympics was $390,000 (Whannel, 1992: 171). By 2008 the US rights alone will be $894m, more than 2000 times higher (Shilbury *et al.*, 1998: 167-8). The 1984 Los Angeles games have been seen as the first profitable games, partly due to the significant increase in television rights since 1980. From the 1992 games the IOC changed its policy of selling television rights, which can now be done well in advance. By early 1996 the IOC had sold the television rights for the 2008 Olympics and even the venue for the 2004 Olympics had been chosen.

FIFA has also increasingly sought to maximise the value of its television rights. Between 1986 and 2006, the cost of non-US World Cup rights had increased from 49m to 1500m Swiss francs. Again this rights inflation has been due to increased competition between broadcasters, but also due to a more aggressively commercial attitude by FIFA in selling rights. In the negotiations for the 2002 and 2006 competitions, instead of selling the European rights directly to broadcasters as they had before through the European Broadcasting Union, FIFA sold the rights to the Kirch group for £1.9 bn (FIFA press release 'World Cup TV rights' 2 July 1996). Although FIFA has strongly expressed the view that television rights should be free to air, and although many European nations have legislation prohibiting exclusive transmission on pay-TV, the sale of rights to a commercial broadcaster introduces a degree of uncertainty about the extent to which European fans will be able to watch some games in the World Cup finals in 2002 and 2006, and, if they can, whether the degree of provision will be more limited than before, given that commercial maximisation of television revenue is based on pay-TV.

The role of FIFA and the IOC in encouraging the growth of sports sponsorship is well documented. The success of the sponsorship basis of both organisations was based on *exclusive* use of trademarks for certain product categories on a worldwide basis, replacing any existing national arrangements in these categories. After Havelange had been elected President of FIFA, he worked with marketing consultant Patrick Nally and Adidas boss Horst Dassler to initiate a sponsorship programme whereby for the 1978 World Cup there were to be six major sponsors (Sugden and Tomlinson, 1998: 86–90). In 1982 Dassler, who was also a member of the IOC until his death in 1987, went on to form the International Sports and Leisure (ISL) group, probably one of the most significant of the major marketing and sports management companies. ISL set up the Olympic Programme (TOP), which again was based on the maximum generation of sponsorship revenue through requiring multinational companies to compete with each other for the right to be the sole sponsor within lucrative product categories (Whannel, 1992: 175). ISL specialised in sponsorship rights, and had specialist divisions in consultancy, events marketing, television, hospitality, licensing, electronic signage and research. However, by April 2001, ISL was declared bankrupt, following its sacking by the IOC in 1995 and a series of extravagant deals, including the ATP men's tennis tour, CART motor racing and most of all the 2002/2006 World Cup television rights deal with the Kirch group, discussed above (Jennings and Wilson, 2001). Perhaps the lesson of the failure of ISL is that the ongoing commercialisation of sport is not a smooth or inevitable process.

One of the most economically significant decisions that FIFA and the IOC make is conferring the privilege of hosting their major competitions: the World Cup and the Olympics. The economic importance of staging such events for cities, regions and nations has now become crucial and it attracts substantial media coverage. Yet there is a conflict between both institutions' expressed preference for a more equitable distribution of venues in the interests of the global development of sport, and the interests of particular constituent organisations (representing either continents, nations or sports), exacerbated by a television-driven commercial context which has its own priorities. Bidding cities and nations are now required to provide a good communications infrastructure and media facilities as a fundamental part of their bid, along with good transportation, stadia facilities, hotel accommodation and security. In addition to all this, television companies and sponsors prefer time zones that are sympathetic to the major television markets, a preference that favours European or North American nations.

The process of awarding the honour of staging the World Cup has become a major issue. Hosting the World Cup has traditionally alternated between Europe and the rest of the world, an arrangement that disproportionately privileges the former. Around the 2006 bid advocates for the main competitors used two positions: that it would be in the interests of soccer globally to stage the World Cup for the first time in Africa (South Africa), and, against this, that the global interests of soccer would best be served through the most successful presentation of the event (Germany and the UK). The South African bid stressed the spin-off effects for other African nations, with the opportunities for neighbouring states to benefit from staging pre-event acclimatisation games between their national teams and those from Europe and Latin America who had qualified. The German and UK bids tended to focus on the best media facilities, security and facilities for spectators, and would be able to host the competition most successfully. Amongst allegations of death threats, the German bid beat the South African one by one vote (Chaudhary, 2000).

The competition to host the Olympics is based on cities rather than nations. The benefits for the host city are debatable. The costs – building and updating of stadia, accommodation, media infrastructure, etc. – are huge. In terms of the profits shown by the city organising committee, these are negligible. Atlanta spent $700m dollars and just about covered its costs. This expenditure is often justified on the basis of the increased business and tourism attracted by the publicity that hosting the Olympic games is supposed to bring, and indeed local businesses may benefit. But the assertion that the local population also benefits is much more difficult to substantiate (see Jefferson Lenskyj 2000).

As these conflicts are settled by voting memberships that are either selected by patronage (the IOC) or by membership of national associations (FIFA), both organisations are democratically unaccountable. The decision to award the 2008 Olympics to Beijing was made by 122 IOC members, the decision to awards the 2006 World Cup to Germany by a 24-member executive committee (comprising 9 from Europe, 4 from Africa, 4 from Asia, 3 from South America, 3 from North and Central America, and 1 from Oceania). Both organisations use transferable votes. Although criteria are set down in advance, the nature of the process means that it is impossible to provide reasons why a particular venue rather than its competitors was selected – leaving a vacuum to be filled by speculation. The 'surprise' decision to award the 2006 Winter Olympics to Turin rather than Sion in Switzerland was widely interpreted as a form of retribution by IOC members against Marc Hodler, the Swiss IOC member responsible for initiating the corruption inquiry.

The membership structure of FIFA and the IOC sets them in a different category from the European Union, whose actions are at least sanctioned by democratically national governments in the last instance. Further, as non-profit organisations, and therefore unlike transnational corporations, FIFA and the IOC are not even responsible to shareholders. Hence there should be no surprise that the media runs extensive scandal stories on FIFA and the IOC. Indeed, if FIFA and the IOC are accountable at all it is to their sponsors. Health care product multinational Johnson and Johnson announced that they decided not to go ahead with sponsorship of the 2002 Salt Lake City Winter Olympics after the bribery scandal (*SporTVision*, Summer: 11).

The more optimistic visions of globalisation tend to focus on its potential for constructing a global community. FIFA and the IOC demonstrate just how tricky this is to attain in practice. The official pronouncements of FIFA and the IOC represent a vision of a world united through sport, yet the recent history of both organisations is characterised by conflict between their stated aims of developing sport globally on the one hand, and using aggressive commercial strategies to pay for this development on the other.

The Olympics opening ceremony usefully illustrates the tensions between the global ideals and increasing commercialisation that characterise the IOC. The opening ceremony at the Atlanta Olympics in 1996 registered sequentially the contradictory identities that the Olympic movement seeks to reconcile. The ceremony began with children dancing in the colours of the Olympic rings, supposedly representing the five continents. The next sequence moved from the global to the national, involving a celebration of a particular image of American culture (here pickup trucks, cheerleaders, marching bands). Then, the local, a mystical sequence invoking Georgia and the south. After the parade, arguably the most memorable image was that of the Parkinson's-disease afflicted Mohammed Ali lighting the

Olympic flame. The non-commercial, spiritual ideals of the Olympic movement evoked in this opening ceremony are rendered through lighting and music that are similar to commercial Hollywood films, emphasised by the appointment of John Williams as composer and musical director (see also Tomlinson, 1996, 2000; Gordon and Sibson, 1998). Further, however FIFA or the IOC attempt to the present themselves as global, the ways in which the Olympic Games and the World Cup are covered will depend on the differing perspective of national sports media (Bernstein, 2000).

The globalisation of sporting cultures

Sport provides a good example of how images of people and events in other parts of the world can be made immediately accessible through the media, contributing to what could be described as a 'global culture'. The economic and political processes described above are having a fundamental, transformative effect on sport wherever it is played or watched in the world. Yet the playing field of global sport is not level. There are number of concerns that are commonly expressed about different aspects of the globalisation of sport. Many are economic. Less profitable sports complain about reduced attendances. Other complaints are to do with the effects that global media sport are having on participation. The decline of West Indies cricket has been blamed on youngsters taking up basketball instead, due to the proximity of the US and the weakening of traditional ties with the Commonwealth. Finally, the globalisation of sport is seen as a threat to a range of traditional values, from fair play through to expression of local and national cultural identities. The idea that the globalisation of sport represents a threat to the economic viability of smaller teams and sports, to levels of participation in national sport, and to traditional sporting and national values, parallels concerns about the effects on national cultures of global media outside sport (for example, over the effects of imported soap operas over indigenous drama). Similarly, the notion that the playing field of global sport is demarcated by inequalities between dominant and subordinate sports, dominate and subordinate nations, is also reflected in wider debates around global culture. This section examines global sport culture within the context of debates on the extent to which cultural imperialism exists in the media in general.

The debate about the extent of domination of the global media by one part of the world (usually the USA) over the rest, is now well established in media and communications research (see Sreberny-Mohammadi, 2000, for a review of it). On the one hand, a number of critics and theorists have argued that the USA has a number of economic advantages in the global media market (Hoskins, McFadyen and Finn, 1997). The main advantage is that the large size of the US market has historically enabled producers to cover their costs at home, meaning that any overseas revenue is pure profit. Because of this, overseas rights can be priced to undercut domestic production in each individual market. Moreover, the US domestic market is heterogeneous, which means that American producers have experience of making programmes which appeal simultaneously to diverse audiences. The USA is home to most of the biggest media corporations in the world, and these corporations have been particularly successful in lobbying US politicians on the need to encourage the export industry through discouraging national overseas content restrictions and production subsidies. US companies have been undergoing a series of mergers and takeovers precisely to give them economic advantages in the global market. For critics, the outcome of these economic advantages is that many nations carry an abundance of US programming which is standardised, homogenised, and formula-led – corresponding to the characteristics of other products, such as Coca-Cola and McDonalds. For many of these critics, this economic imbalance between the USA and other nations leads to a form of cultural imperialism, whereby the programmes promote a set of values conducive to US capitalism.

Yet others have argued that the global trade in media is much more diverse and heterogeneous than that. Firstly, the trade in media products is by no means one-way – that is, from the USA to the rest. Whereas the economic importance of the US is beyond dispute, there are also other significant producer nations who export to other markets with which they share cultural, linguistic or historical links (for example, Brazil exports telenovelas to Portugal, Egypt exports soap operas throughout the Arab-speaking world). And whereas national broadcasters are happy to fill daytime schedules with cheap, imported programming, ratings research has shown that national audiences prefer home-produced drama (Tracey, 1988). Although a majority of the biggest transnational media corporations are based in the US, a significant number are based in Europe and Japan.

Further, a central theme of the cultural imperialism thesis – that economic dominance of US media entails the successful proliferation of American values, is problematic. The cultural imperialist argument is consistent with Marxist theories of ideology that treat media audiences as dupes, uncritically adopting the values of the media which they encounter. Drawing on different types of audience research, critics have argued that far from being cultural dupes, audiences actively construct their own meanings around imported programmes.

How does sport fit into this debate about the economic dominance of the American media and their cultural and social effects? The *Sociology of Sport Journal* published a number of articles in the early 1990s on whether recent trends in global sport constituted either Americanisation, or variously, mundialisation, modernisation or globalisation (see Maguire, 1990; Klein, 1991, for an example of the former interpretation, and Wagner, 1990; Guttmann, 1991; or McKay and Miller, 1991 for the latter). The debate has continued in that journal, the *Journal of Sport and Social Issues* and elsewhere up to the present (Donnelly, 1996; Guttmann 1993, 1994; Harvey and Houle, 1994; Harvey, Rail and Thibault, 1996; Houlihan, 1994; Maguire, 1994; Miller *et al.*, 2001; Rowe *et al.*, 1994; Rowe, 1996).

The late 1980s/early 1990s was a crucial time in the history of American media sport. It was a moment when the domestic market was widely perceived to have reached maturity. A sign of this recognition was when the big three networks refused to pay any more for sports rights – although this strategy was undermined by Fox (Bellamy, 1998: 75). So the major leagues recognised that expansion could only come from marketing these sports overseas. The mixed success of these conscious initiatives to export American sports on other nation's sporting cultures are enlightening in demonstrating on the one hand the economic advantages of American companies, but on the other hand the limits of marketing and media.

There are two different strategies that can be invoked in order to operate transnationally. The first is to market a standardised product globally, using advertising strategies which may differ between markets to a greater or lesser extent. The second is to follow the famous maxim 'act globally, think locally', which involves the indigenisation of the product, possibly through partnerships with local companies. Attempts to market the major American sports have typically combined both strategies.

Baseball

Baseball has often been identified as the archetypal American game, apparently 'invented' in a Cooperstown cow pasture by General Abner Doubleday in 1839. Putting aside arguments about the mythical status of this account, the story is important in terms of the construction of American national identity, locating the origins of the game within a masculine, military context, differentiated from other bat and ball games, particularly rounders. Since these origins baseball has occupied a central place as an American sport.

By the 1990s the US market for baseball as well as for the other major sports had achieved maturity, and expansion could only be found overseas. By 1999 Major League Baseball-International reported that it had quadrupled overseas income over five years to c. $25–30 million (although this was still less than 10 per cent of the $345 million generated by the US rights). Baseball is sold to around 200 countries, and is particularly strong in the Pacific Rim and in Latin America.

The overseas sales success of baseball is uneven, however, illustrating the limits of the power of marketing. The most lucrative overseas market is Japan, where baseball has been the national sport since between the wars. If there has been an 'Americanisation' of sport in

Japan it hasn't happened with the recent marketing activities of MLB-I, but over a much longer period of time between the 1870s and the 1930s. Baseball was introduced to Japan in the 1870s by US educators, but as early as the 1890s success by Japanese teams over the nation which invented it was represented as an assertion of national identity. During the modernisation of Japanese identity in the 1920s and 1930s, the game was 'Japanised' as 'Chinese character equivalents were invented to replace its foreign terminology' (Watts, 1998: 187). After the war US occupation forces were concerned about the nationalistic overtones of Japanese baseball, and encouraged the playing of soccer instead (Watts, 1999: 187). Baseball remains the most popular sport in Japan, although the meanings of the game have historically depended on the popularity of American culture in Japan. At one moment, baseball represents a love for Americana, at another, baseball can represent the ultimate assertion of Japanese identity.

What can be learnt from the experience of Japanese baseball? First the imperial legacy of US nineteenth-century expansionism is clearly evident, although according to an influential account baseball transplanted so successfully because it coincided with traditional religious, aesthetic or philosophical principles (Whiting, 1977).

It has long been noted that Latin and Central American nations have lost their best baseball players to the US because of higher wages (Klein, 1991). However, a new development is the presence of Asian players in MLB, which increases the sport's attractiveness within the players' home market. Hideo Nomo broke new ground by leaving Japan for the LA Dodgers during 1995, followed closely by Hideki Irabu's departure for the New York Yankees (Watts, 1999; Mayeda, 1999). Later, the presence of pitcher Chan Ho Park in the LA Dodgers enables Major League Baseball International to sell rights to all the team's games to Korean broadcaster INCHON TV for $3m over three years, a tenfold increase over the previous revenue derived from this market ('Baseball continues its global roll', *Sports TV Report* 35, 31 May 1999).

MLB's international marketing operation, MLB-I, has employed a different strategy in Europe, which is seen as more resistant. In order to try to develop markets for the game in future through encouraging participation, MLB-I has produced its weekly *Baseball Max!* series, introducing new viewers to the game, and also educational materials ('Baseball continues its global roll' *Sports TV Report* 35, 31 May 1999).

Although Major League Baseball-International has done well to increase its global marketing activities, its success in the Pacific Rim and Latin America, as opposed to Europe, demonstrates the limits of the media in creating a market. MLB-I's have been most successful in those nations where baseball is already popular and is played.

Football

One of the earliest successful attempts by the NFL to market US sport internationally occurred in the UK in the 1980s, when their collaboration with the brewers Anheuser-Busch led to the regular screening of US football from 1982. Audiences rose to over 6 million for the 1987 Super Bowl (comparable to the soccer FA Cup final). The screening of NFL was complemented by support for leagues in the UK and Europe, in one case as a result of Anheuser-Busch sponsorship. However, it seems that the American product appealed to audiences more than the indigenous European gridiron. From 1991 the World League of American Football (WLAF) was set up using teams from the US, Canada and Europe, but collapsed in 1998 through disastrous US viewing figures. After Fox's purchase of the NFL rights, the WLAF was relaunched in 1995 using European teams only, renamed NFL Europe in 1998. By 1999, the rights to screening the NFL in the UK were held by BSkyB. An analysis of the advertisements carried during the latter's coverage of the 1999 Super Bowl, featuring NASDAQ and various blue chip companies, such as Dell computers, suggests that whereas in the 1980s the NFL, its sponsors and Channel 4 attempted to build a mass audience for the sport, by the end of 1990s ambitions for the size of the audience US football could attract in the UK were much more limited, and instead the sport was marketed to an affluent 'niche' audience.

What I would like to argue here is that the success of US football in the UK in the 1980s was dependent on the context in which it was consumed. Maguire (1990, 1993a) argues that the typical consumer for American football in the 1980s was young, male and affluent. He argues that this consumer was perceived as not having a sport they could call their own at that time. Channel 4's presentation of American football fitted in well dominant ideologies around social mobility, individualised consumption, entrepreneurship and modernisation, in a context of long-term, irreversible decline for the major UK spectator sport, soccer, which was afflicted by decaying stadia, crowd violence and an unglamorous, down-at-heel image. American football was not so much *pushed* by the NFL and Anheuser-Busch on to the UK, but *pulled* by the emergence of a new television channel and independent production company seeking to fill a vacuum from a specific social group. Equally, after the professionalisation of the UK sport after the Hillsborough disaster in the 1990s, and what many observers have seen as the yuppification of soccer, entailing corporate hospitality and the launch of Premier League football in 1992, it is reasonable to argue that the affluent audiences who were attracted to US football in the 1980s moved on to soccer. In other words, when UK sport was sufficiently professionalised for the UK middle classes, they rejected imported alternatives.

Basketball

Basketball was invented at an YMCA in Springfield, Massachusetts in 1891 (Dunning, Maguire and Pearton, 1993: 16). The National Basketball Association (NBA) is widely recognised as having achieved a major turnaround over the last couple of decades, but by the early 1990s had gone as far as it could in the USA. NBA International signed television and marketing deals with national broadcasters and with regional broadcasters in particular regions (Star, ESPN International, SkySport). Nike and Reebok promote NBA through their marketing of black basketball stars. NBA international merchandising amounted to $300 million.

Unlike many other multinational corporations that engage in an operational strategy known as global localization in an attempt to blend into the local culture and effectively become a part of the indigenous ethnoscape, the NBA explicitly promotes itself as a signifier of cultural difference. (Jackson and Andrews, 1999a: 35; see also Jackson and Andrews, 1999b)

What conclusions can we draw from a comparative analysis of the major league's attempts to market their games overseas? Attempts to promote the adoption of these as *world* sports to match the success of soccer through *indigenisation* has met with limited success so far. Rather these sports have been successfully marketed precisely by selling their 'Americanness'. Further where the export of televised American sport has been successful it has required as a precondition the existence of specific groups for whom the US has a specific meaning in relation to national domestic culture. The significance of American football in the 1980s for British yuppies, as of the importance of Michael Jordan for New Zealand youngsters, is located within a complex dynamic in which the marketing strategies of transnational corporations negotiate with the social relations that characterise particular groups in particular markets.

What this discussion has shown is that the success of the international marketing of sport is not *guaranteed* in advance, however dominant the transnational companies might appear to be. Rather it is conditional on the specific social dynamics and relational context through which the export of sport occurs, and this depends on the characteristics of national and local markets.

There is another way in which the Americanisation of sport can be viewed, which is to suggest that it is not so much important in terms of the imposition of particular sports but rather in terms of the revolution in business methods that have been described above. The USA has a historical advantage over Europe in the commercialisation of sport. It is not just that the US media followed a commercial model rather than Europe's public service model. It is also that US teams were generally more entrepreneurial from the beginning, while sport in Europe had more community-based forms of ownership. Most of the major transnational media companies are based in the USA. It has a huge domestic audience. Innovative forms of sponsorship and marketing have been initiated by US-based companies, such as Nike. But whether 'Americanisation' is useful as any more than a short-hand descriptive term indicating the benefits of a historical advantage is open to doubt – often the term is used in a xenophobic way to try to construct positive national identities.

In looking at globalisation from a cultural perspective rather than from just an economic one, it can be seen that globalisation is not just the outcome of the activities of transnational companies – it is much more complex than that. As well as looking at the globalisation of capital, it is also important to note the globalisation of people, or migration. It is here particularly that concerns about contemporary cultural imperialism lack a sense of history. One of the key problems of seeing the export of mediated US sport in terms of cultural impe-rialism is its ahistorical perspective, which does not take into account the post-colonial context in which media sport is imported. Sreberny-Mohammadi (2000: 95–6) has argued that many critiques of cultural imperialism which focus on the recent role of the media ignore

> the many deep and diverse cultural effects of imperialism itself,
> including the export of religion, educational systems and values,
> European languages, and administrative practices, all of which
> have long ago and irretrievably altered the cultural milieu of the
> colonized.

Sport can be considered to be one of these 'cultural effects of imperi-alism'. Most sports were codified and diffused through the British empire from the nineteenth century. For example, cricket was played in the Victorian public schools and disseminated as the alumni of those schools took up posts as administrators, and played as part of the 'civilising mission'. Thus cricket is played predominantly in those countries which used to be part of the British Empire. However, though the sport may have been the 'imperial game', there is nothing intrinsically imperialist about the rules of the game, and the sport was indigenised in Britain's former colonies. C. L. R. James's famous book *Beyond a Boundary* (1963) discusses the role of cricket in life in the West Indies as both an imperial legacy and an expression of resistance. In India, according to Appadurai, 'to account for the central place of cricket in the Indian imagination, one must understand how cricket links gender, the nation, fantasy and bodily excitement' (1995: 44). At the same time, the relationship between cricket and post-colonial national identities is both complex and problematic, as studies of the sport in Sri Lanka (Ismail, 1997) and South Africa (Farred, 1997) have shown.

Conclusion

At the moment, any sports fan who closely follows news reports about what is happening to their team or to their sport will have, perhaps unwittingly, become an expert on globalisation and its effects. This chapter has argued that whereas sport has been global since the late nineteenth century, the present phase of globalisation is inextricably related to the role of television, leading to a shift in the economics of global sport from an industrial to a post-industrial structure. In pursuing their stated sporting and social ideals, FIFA and the IOC have played a fundamental if problematic role in this shift. But globalisation should not just be understood from an economic or political perspective, focusing on the agency of transnational companies in conjunction with administrative bodies. What is also crucial to understanding the globalisation of sport is the ways in which these processes are lived and experienced in local contexts, to understand the cultural as well as the economic and political dynamics of globalisation.

|4|

Media, sport, and national identities

It is difficult to understate the importance of national identity to the media presentation of sport. It is almost taken for granted that media coverage of international sporting competitions, such as the Olympics or the men's soccer World Cup, will assume spectators' main interest to be in the athletes or teams representing their own nation. Indeed, for many this may be their only interest. Even national sports events, like the Super Bowl, reinforce a sense of national community, marking regular festive breaks from everyday routine, and linking domestic viewing rituals with the larger 'imagined community' of the nation.

Further, sport events can provide the arena for the representation of celebratory images of nationalism, even 'multiculturalism'. For example, after South Africa's victory at the 1995 Rugby World Cup, which it had hosted, television pictures were transmitted around the world of Nelson Mandela celebrating in the Springboks shirt. On him, its traditional connotations of Afrikaaner nationalism were transformed to symbolise the ANC's policies of reconciliation (Nauright, 1997; Farred, 1997; Black and Nauright, 1998; Booth, 1999; Crawford, 1999).

On the other hand, national media presentation of international sporting events is often characterised by stereotyping of other nations. Some of this stereotyping borders on xenophobia through explicit, derogatory references to national dress, food, culture, etc. –

the English tabloid press being the most infamous offender in this respect. And a more pervasive form of stereotyping can also be identified in the attribution of styles of play and temperament to individuals and teams according to supposed national characteristics.

The relationship between media, sport and national identity is thus obvious, but it is also extremely complex. This chapter attempts to unpack the different ways in which it can be conceptualised.

While sport on the media provides a rich source of representations of national identity, sport as a commodity demonstrates that the idea of national identity is becoming increasingly problematic in a global context. A growing number of cricket, rugby union and soccer players are choosing to play for nations in which they were neither born nor have lived on the purely pragmatic basis that this will enhance their career prospects. The media can encourage fans to identity with different nations at different times. In the UK, radio and television commentary often assumes that the English sports fan will support England in national soccer competitions, Great Britain in the Olympics, and Europe in golf's Ryder Cup. The media encourages this promiscuity: allegiances are surprisingly transferable. If there are no English representatives in an international competition, the English media will transfer its allegiance to competitors from Wales, Scotland or Ireland. There are limits to this flexibility, however: the Scottish media tends not to support England.

The lesson from media sport is that whereas the rhetoric of national identity is about uncomplicated allegiance to a nation based, singly or variously, on place of residence, place of birth or parental lineage, support for a nation is in fact surprisingly provisional, and easily transferable. The indications are that the ongoing commodification and globalisation of sport is influencing the cultural and social significance of national identities. This chapter indicates some of these effects.

According to the 'borderless world' version of globalisation (p. 51), the nation-state is withering away in the heat of global economic imperatives. Postmodernists argue that new communications technologies will replace place-defined collective identities with 'communities of interest' that have 'no sense of place' (Meyrowitz,

1985). But sport demonstrates how inadequate these perspectives are. Over the last twenty years or so sport has been at the forefront of new media developments: from direct broadcast by satellite, cable and digital television, through to web broadcasting and inter-active television. And far from undermining national differences, the economics of media sport reinforce them. The global marketing of media is based on the differentiation of national markets: the commercial maximisation of sport globally depends on sales to new markets at negligible new production and distribution costs. Hence the significance of the emerging science of virtual advertising (the digital insertion of virtual advertisements into live footage to approximate actual advertising), which enables national broadcast-ers to sell advertising space within their own markets and also to transcend nationally specific advertising restrictions, for example on tobacco.

National public service and commercial terrestrial broadcasters have always encouraged viewers' identification with national teams or individuals through the framing of their coverage and sports jour-nalism. But pay-TV and pay-per-view broadcasters likewise recog-nise the value of identification with the national community in their promos for particular services and events.

So we could say that national identity is not only central to media sport but that aspects of the global media economy have tended to reinforce those forms of national identity. Yet there are also signs that the identification of fans with sports stars representing their national community is problematic. Something is happening to national iden-tities. It is not necessary to subscribe to the idea that globalisation entails the demise of nation-states to recognise that the reproduction of national cultural identities is undergoing fundamental change. In order to address the question of what is happening to national iden-tities as constructed through media sport in the context of globalisa-tion, the relationship between media, sport and national identity needs to be examined before discussing how it has changed under globalization. It is not a case of national identity versus globalisation, but rather that globalisation seems both to reinforce national identi-ties and to undermine them.

By definition a general chapter on the way that media and sport work to construct national identities is nearly impossible. This is because although the nation-state is now the universal form of political organisation, at the same time the reinforcement of symbolic difference from one another is fundamental to the way in which nation-states are represented. Hence there is always a limit to the extent to which conclusions about one nation-state are transferable to another. Even in the case of 'stateless nations' – for example Scotland and Catalonia, which certainly express their cultural identity through sport – there are few similarities in the way they do this.

National identities as social–historical constructions

National identity is a social–historical construction. Anderson (1991) situates the replacement of religion by nationalism as the dominant meaning-system historically, coterminous with a range of developments, including print–capitalism. Further, just as national identities are constructed, they are continually being reconstructed. The press and broadcasting do not just reflect national identities, they have played a major historical role in their constitution and transformation. Mercer (1992) has argued that the role of the newspaper in the historical constitution of the nation is based on its status as quotidian, ephemeral, everyday and routine. He argues that it is important to conceive of the nation as habitus and that therefore

> we can propose a concept of the nation not as a static structure, a container of dominant ideologies, a simple 'invention' or, indeed a 'myth', but rather in terms of the rituals, daily practices, techniques, institutions, manners and customs which enable the nation to be thinkable, inhabitable, communicable and therefore governable. (Mercer, 1992: 27)

Anderson's thesis on the role of print–capitalism in the constitution of national identities also focuses on the quotidian. He ascribes to the media a fundamental role in the constitution of nations as 'imagined communities', in the form of daily newspaper reading:

> each communicant is well aware that the ceremony he performs is being replicated simultaneously by thousands (or millions) of others of whose existence he is confident, yet of whose identity he has not the slightest notion. Furthermore, this ceremony is incessantly repeated at daily or half-daily intervals throughout the calendar. What more vivid figure for the secular, historically-clocked, imagined community can be envisioned? (Anderson, 1991: 35)

For Anderson, the ritual of newspaper reading is part of the social organisation of 'empty, homogeneous time' characteristic of modernity: empty because it is contrasted with the 'sacred time' of previous societies based on religious belief, homogeneous because it is uniformly measured by clock or calendar and is unaffected by the varying significance of events. The key word in this extract is 'simultaneously': the simultaneous consumption of newspapers constructs an imagined nation whose individuals may be distant but contained within finite boundaries. Hence the idea of clock-time is significant in terms of national identity because it foregrounds the routine, the everyday, the banal (see also Billig, 1995; Brookes, 1988).

Anderson's comments are important in understanding how sport, and media coverage of sport, have contributed to the formation of national identity through making a psychological connection between the everyday life of the individual and the wider abstract category of the nation. It is easy to see, for example, how first newspaper coverage and then televised broadcasts of sport can be seen to contribute to a sense of shared belonging. What is particularly important is how national identification through sport can be seen to be situated in the mundane, the ritual, and the everyday.

However, Anderson's comments can only form a starting-point for discussions of national identity and media sport. The broad historical and geographical sweep of this work tends to sideline the important differences in the ways in which national identity is constructed. It is not enough to know that media sport plays a role in the construction of national identities, we need to know what role media sport plays in the formation of different types of national identity. Whereas the significance of Anderson's work lies in the argument about the constructed nature of national identities, the impression is given that these identities are fixed, static and consensual. What, for example, about individuals who decline this invitation to identify with the nation through sport, or conversely, those who because of their backgrounds are encouraged to identify with more than one nation? These considerations are significant in the context of conflicts between 'stateless nations' and nation-states, and in terms of men being much more likely to identify with the nation than women, particularly through sport. It is important to note, for example, that even in the sociology of sport, an academic field that tends to be dominated by men anyway, the interest in sport and national identity is an almost exclusively male terrain. Even critical accounts can tend to prioritise national identity over other forms of identity.

If we are to understand the media's role in the formation of national identities, then we need to have a more dynamic theory than Anderson is able to produce. For this, I want to turn to the broader types of theory of identity acquisition associated with recent developments in cultural studies. Hall has argued that late twentieth-century cultural and social theory has problematised the notion of the unitary, 'Cartesian' subject which underpins conventional discussions of cultural identity (Hall, 1992). He argues that the cultural identities people have are not fixed and unified, but contingent, in process, and potentially contradictory. In the context of a discussion of the 'politics of living identity through difference', Hall argues that 'all of us are composed of multiple social identities, not of one . . . we are all complexly constructed through different categories, of different antagonisms' (Hall, 1991b: 57). National identity is one social identity among others. Further, in the new phase of globalisation characterised by postcolonial migration, this has led to the increased visibility of 'hybrid' and 'diasporic' identities (Hall, 1991a) – sport has a major role to play in the production of both of these (see below, p. 103).

The crucial point is that whereas national identity is represented as fixed, natural and eternal, it is continually in process. National identities are not just imagined once, but are continually reinvented. And they need to be understood within a dynamic relationship with identities based on gender, sexuality, locality, ethnicity, region, religion, etc.

Hence it is important to distinguish between how national identities are represented (that is, as timeless and immutable) and how they are produced (that is, as the result of a continual process of transformation). Hegemonic representations of national identity are based on notions of consensus, a common interest amongst those living within the nation, a shared cultural heritage, and a seamless history characterised by continuity and tradition – and difference in all of these respects from other nations. Sport has played a major role in this invention of tradition. Mythical accounts of the origins of some sports serve to define those sports as particularly belonging to specific nations, social classes, etc. The popular myth that William Webb Ellis invented rugby by picking up the ball and running with it at Rugby School in 1823 was originated in the 1890s, and served to locate the origins of rugby within the English public school system, at a time when the administrative hegemony of English middle-class values was coming under attack from the professionalism of Northern rugby and the more cross-class pragmatism of Welsh rugby.

However, national identities are continually contested – hegemonic representations define national identities in ways which reproduce dominant class, ethnic, regional, religious or gender interests. National identities in media sport should not be seen as fixed and unproblematic, but as continually contested, particularly in the current phase of globalisation. As broadcasters and governments alike aggressively promote the importance of national sporting success, television sport tends to reinforce differences through representing a sense of national self-identity. The selection of particular sports rather than others as symbols of national identity, of particular stars rather than others as epitomising aspects of national character, are directly related to these struggles over national identity. However, these representations are often highly gendered and ethnocentric, reflecting tensions between traditional and modern, exclusive and inclusive visions of the nation.

Media sport and national identity in the USA: the Super Bowl

Although the role of sport in the construction of national identity has been a widely researched area, there has been relatively little that explicitly addresses the construction of national identity through sport in the USA. Whereas sports studies has become a growth area in American universities, when it comes to identity issues researchers tend to be more interested in issues of race and gender (Bairner, 2001: 91). For example, Jay Coakley's massive 600-page *Sport in Society*, at the time of writing in its seventh edition, has chapters on a whole range of social issues, including race, class and gender, but restricts nationalism to a few index entries (1998). Yet sport in the USA provides a very good example of the more banal ways in which it plays a role in the construction of national identity.

There can scarcely be a better example than the Super Bowl. Since its inauguration in 1967, the National Football League's Super Bowl has provided the paradigm example of television's role in the increasing commodification of sport. In the US many of the highest rating television events ever are Super Bowls, with the 1996 game between the Dallas Cowboys and the Pittsburgh Steelers peaking at 138.5 million viewers. Super Bowl parties are thrown as highways and shopping malls are emptied (Wenner, 1989: 157). Super Bowl Sunday has become a festive ritual linking households with the abstract community of the nation through a shared viewing experience, providing an ideal opportunity for the articulation of hegemonic representations of American values (Wenner, 1989). The Super Bowl provided a prestigious showcase for new advertisements from blue-chip companies. The fees that broadcasters have commanded have been estimated at $1m for a 30-second spot in 1995, increasing to $2m in 2000. And competition for the broadcasting rights to the package of which the Super Bowl forms a part is fierce, the cost of rights escalating exponentially with each new contract negotiated. The package the NFL sold to ABC, CBS and Fox in 1998 amounted to $2.2 billion a year. American Football also provides one of the earliest examples of how the rules of sport have been modified as a result of the growing economic power of television – it was as long ago as 1958 that the television time-out was introduced to provide extra spots for advertisers.

The Super Bowl occupies a regular place in the national calendar, usually on the first Sunday in February. This national festival is staged by a different city each year, which gives local authorities and companies a lucrative opportunity to market the city and the surrounding area to tourists and business. The build-up to the match starts up to two weeks before the event. The NFL, the two participating teams, the host city's organising committee, sponsors, and other interested parties all provide the media with stories through press conferences, controlled access to the players, and other stage-managed events (Schwartz, 1997).

Promotion constitutes a crucial element of Super Bowl coverage. A video segment introducing Sky Sports' presentation of Fox coverage of the 1999 Super Bowl between Denver Broncos and Atlanta Falcons typifies how television heightens viewer interest in sporting events through intensifying conflict between the participants. The narration introduced the teams as having in different ways confounded the expectations of the pundits in reaching the Super Bowl: 'They said the Atlanta Falcons couldn't beat their long-term divisional rivals, the San Francisco 49ers . . . standing in their way are the defending champions, the Denver Broncos, the team the experts said could never repeat their success.' The segment then spotlights the key players as their surnames cover half the screen in bold, shaded capitals, running from right to left across slow-motion action and close-ups, filled with images of flames. As Denver's Bill Romanowski is featured, the narration defines him as 'maybe the meanest player to wear an NFL uniform. If he's got your number, your number's up'. Finally, the main angle: for Dan Reeves, head coach of the Atlanta Falcons, 'it's payback time'. Reeves had previously been fired from his job with the Broncos over a falling-out with retiring hero John Elway. 'Revenge is in the air' – announced the narrator. This video segment framed the game between the Broncos and the Falcons as a contest between men motivated by personal challenges and vendettas, a contest to be resolved through controlled violence. The timbre and depth of the narrator's voice, the brooding *Star Wars*-style synthesised orchestral and choral music, the pace of the editing, the use of names, all recall action or sci-fi movie trailers.

Video segments are used to promote the Super Bowl through innovative use of editing, computer-generated effects, sound and music. By contrast, television presentation of the game typifies that of other sporting events in relying on conventional tried-and-tested techniques. Television presentation is anchored by a main camera position that pans and zooms, following the action, supplemented by a proliferation of fixed and mobile cameras. Most of the presentation still follows the accepted convention in covering the action from one side of an imaginary line that runs between the goalposts. American Football is well known for its stop-start action – the ball is 'in play' considerably less than similar sports (Real, 1989). Breaks are filled by detailed analysis of replays and statistics, and of course, advertisements. Close-ups of players are also regularly featured, although American football is different from other sports in that the protective headgear used prevents television from conveying the player's emotions through the demonstration of facial expressions – almost as if to compensate, the aggressive or celebratory gestures performed by the players appear exaggerated.

As has been argued above, though, it is not just that national identity is constructed through media coverage of sporting events, but that a particular type of national identity is constructed through that coverage. Women are largely absent from Super Bowl telecasts, visible only as cheerleaders or as entertainers in the half-time show. The generic conventions through which television promotes, covers and reports the Super Bowl reinforces the status of American football as arguably the most effective sport in reproducing hegemonic representations of masculinity (Trujillo, 1995), affirming the conclusion reached by Real (1975: 42) that:

North American professional football is an aggressive, strictly regulated team game fought between males who use both violence and technology to gain control of property for the economic gain of individuals within a nationalistic entertainment context.

Other sports, sporting events and personalities can provide vehicles for the projection of various meanings around US national identity – a number of studies analysing the significance of major sporting celebrities in terms of nation, 'race' and gender will be referred to in Chapters 5 and 6. Why the Super Bowl is particularly important in terms of American national identity is that it provides the focus for an unparalleled national ritual, and at the same time projects a particular image of national identity that is both rigidly gendered and heavily commodified.

Media sport and national identities in the UK

The construction of national identities in the UK through media coverage of sport can be conceptualised in two interrelated ways. Firstly, representations of national self-identity can be identified in, for example, media inquests of the failure of a national sports team and the extent to which this failure can be explained in terms of the national condition. Secondly, national identity is constructed through representations of difference from other national identities. Through the negative stereotyping of other nations, a positive sense of national self-identity is implied.

Writing about the English, Hall argues:

To be English is to know yourself in relation to the French, and the hot-blooded Mediterraneans, and the passionate, traumatized Russian soul. You go round the entire globe: when you know what everyone else is, then you are what they are not. *Identity is always, in that sense, a structured representation which only achieves its positive through the narrow eye of the negative* (Hall, 1991a: 21, my emphasis).

Although English national identity could be said to have been experiencing an intense post-colonial sense of national crisis, the argument that national self-identity is predominantly defined in opposition to the identity of other nations is generalisable. National identity is usually constructed through establishing differences between 'us' and 'them' (Brookes, 1999).

Research on the role of media specifically in the construction of national identities in the UK has tended to focus on men's soccer, and particularly major international men's soccer tournaments such as the World Cup and the European Championship. A number of studies of televised soccer have foregrounded issues of national and racial stereotyping in the coverage of these competitions. Two early studies emphasise the importance of scene-setting: McArthur (1975) on television listings magazines and Tudor (1975) on discussion panels. Nowell-Smith (1979) examines televisual codes and conventions governing coverage of the 1978 World Cup in Argentina in relation to contemporary issues in international politics. Wren-Lewis and Clarke (1983) analyse television coverage of the 1982 World Cup in Spain in the context of the Falklands War. Tudor (1992), focusing on England and Cameroon at the 1990 World Cup, examines the ways in which television, and particularly commentary, represents race and national identity through narrative and stereotyping.

More recently, research on the relationship between media, soccer and national identities has focused on newspapers. Blain and O'Donnell have analysed press representations of national identities in international competitions across a range of European newspapers (Blain, Boyle and O'Donnell, 1993; O'Donnell, 1994; Blain and O'Donnell, 1998). Two research projects have compared the construction of national identity in English and German press coverage of the Euro '96 competitions. Analysing newspaper coverage across Europe, Blain and O'Donnell (1998) argue that there is a fundamental difference between the reporting of Euro '96 in Britain and Portugal – 'the two European countries with the worst post-imperialist hangovers in Europe' – and the rest of Europe, including Germany. This difference can be explained in terms of the degree of political modernity, so that in Britain/England sporting success or failure comes to stand in for the success or failure of the nation in general, in the rest of Europe sporting success or failure is only one way of being and does not come to stand in for the nation as a whole. Maguire, Poulton and Possamai (1999a, 1999b) argue that this difference can be understood in terms of a historical perspective, in which English press reporting is characterised by a 'wilful nostalgia' with persistent reference to its military and imperial past, where German press reporting is characterised by eschewing historical references in favour of assertions of contemporary economic and political superiority (see also Garland and Rowe, 1999).

In this section I want to examine the interrelated ways in which the media coverage of sport in England represents English national identity: firstly, through representing other nations and secondly through representing Englishness itself.

On 24 June 1996, on the day of the semi-final between England and Germany in the men's soccer European Championships, the popular English tabloid the *Daily Mirror* declared 'Football war on Germany'. On in its front page it ran the headline 'ACHTUNG SURRENDER. For you Fritz, ze Euro '96 Championship is over'. This notorious front page has been frequently reproduced as paradigmatic of tabloid xenophobia. This representation draws on the same imagery through which France and Germany are stereotypically represented in the English tabloid press, harking back to Europhobic classics like the Sun's 'Up yours Delors!' campaign (aimed at Jacques Delors, the former president of the EU, [see Hardt-Mautner 1995]). It is also relevant that Euro '96 took place just after the outbreak of the 'beef war' between Britain and the EU (Brookes, 1999).

What is most significant about this episode is perhaps the widespread negative reaction from the public, other media organisations, advertisers and regulators, all of whom moved swiftly to denounce 'Achtung Surrender' as an example of unacceptable nationalism. The outcry forced the editor of the *Daily Mirror*, Piers Morgan, into an apology. The 'Achtung Surrender' episode was an example of competing discourses around English national identity, in which really the dominant discourse was that of the shocked response. Lord Wakeham, chair of the Press Complaints Commission issued warnings to the press to 'temper nationalistic language' in their coverage of France '98 (Ahmed, 1998).

How about the ways in which English national self-identity is represented through media coverage of sport? I would like to suggest that there are two interrelated ways in which this occurs. First, through the ways in which players, coaches and administrators are represented. Second, through the ways in which the English people are represented through the media as television viewers, fans and hooligans.

First, the ways in which the players are represented. I would argue that there are two interrelated frames through which English performance is understood in the media. One is that English sport is in a state of terminal decline. On 23 August 1999, after the defeat of England by New Zealand in the test series, the *Sun* ran a front page that could be described as paradigmatic of how English sport is represented in its own media. It was an adaptation of a spoof obituary place in the *Sporting Times* in 1882, following an English defeat by Australia. Against a black background, the following epitaph appeared around a photograph of burning bails:

OFFICIAL
Worst team in the world
ENGLISH CRICKET
1744–1999
'In affectionate remembrance of English cricket which died at The Oval, 22nd August 1999. Deeply lamented by a large circle of sorrowing friends and acquaintances, R. I. P.'

Here I want to examine a particular discourse that we can identify as the state of English sport. This is a nostalgic discourse of national decline, in which the decline of 'our' sports teams mirrors the decline of a world order in which Britain was a major imperialist power. A familiar narrative can be identified across English media coverage of cricket and soccer particularly. The story goes that England gave these sports to the world, and that therefore England should naturally be able to beat other nations. Media sports coverage evaluates the performances of present managers, captains and players in relation to those that represent this assumed golden age, and usually finds them wanting. In the case of soccer this imagined golden age lasted the length of England's victory over West Germany in the World Cup Final at Wembley in 1966. Critcher argued that this victory 'disguised the deep-rooted problems in the English game' by 'perpetuating the belief that success on the international stage could be achieved without radically altering our ways' (1994: 90). The 'myth of 1966' was reinvigorated by England's progress to the semi-finals at the Italia '90 World Cup (only to be beaten by Germany after a penalty shoot-out), the coverage of the death the captain of the England 1966 side Bobby Moore in 1993, and England's hosting of the Euro 2000 championship, which again saw England beaten by Germany in the semi-finals after a penalty shoot-out. The latter tournament was marked by the release of the official England song 'Football's coming home', written and performed by Ian Broudie of 'Britpop' band the Lightning Seeds with comedians David Baddiel and Frank Skinner, which – particularly through its line about 'thirty years of hurt'– renewed the 'myth of 1966' for a new generation of young men, defined by the growth of 'new lad' culture based around magazines like *Loaded* (Carrington, 1998: 110). The England soccer team manager in particular bears the brunt of this type of comparison from the tabloids. In his analysis of UK press coverage of England managers in the 1980s and early 1990s, Wagg (1991: 237) concluded:

> In reality, England is a country like many others and the English football team is a football team like many others ... But the Sun, a powerful definer, has created an atavistic fantasy in which it cannot be known, and merely to suggest it is contempt of court. That being so, it is unlikely that 'the tabloids' will in the foreseeable future find anyone who is good enough to manage the England football team. Any incumbent will instead bear the brunt of their oblique, post-imperial British racism, which says 'our team must be gutless if it can't beat that lot'.

The paradigmatic example of this was on 18 June 1992 after England finished bottom of their group at the European Championship, losing to Sweden. 'SWEDEN 2 TURNIPS 1' ran the headline alongside a montage of manager Graham Taylor's face superimposed on a turnip. This conclusion could equally be extended to cover the managerships of Glenn Hoddle (1996–99) and Kevin Keegan (1999–2000), and to the cricket equivalent of the manager, the captain.

Analyses of the media representations of English national identity in soccer coverage tend to agree that the stereotypical values of English soccer are based on honesty, commitment, effort, hard work and stamina. These values are stereotypically constructed by contrast to the stereotypical sporting values of other parts of the world, both positive (the 'Latin flair' of South American players) and negative ('cheating foreigners'). According to this account, success will be dependent on the extent to which the present team representing England lives up to these values. In a second round match during the France 1998 World Cup, England lost on penalties after extra time to Argentina, this despite Michael Owen having scored one of the goals of the tournament, and despite the rest of the team struggling for more than an hour with ten men after David Beckham had been sent off for kicking out at an opponent just after half time. The reaction of the English media was to pick out a scapegoat, as they had in the 1990 World Cup and Euro '96 semi-final defeats against Germany. On that occasion it was the players who had missed their penalties: Stuart Pearce, Chris Waddle, and Gareth Southgate. After the match against Argentina in 1998, despite having a similar scapegoat avail-able – David Batty had missed the penalty – it was David Beckham who bore the brunt of unprecedented hostile press criticism. The point most relevant here is the extent to which this criticism related to issues around national identity:

10 Heroic Lions, One Stupid Boy (*Mirror*, 1 July 1998).
Beckham's silly little, smart little kick at his opponent was what's wrong with the national character. This Gaultier-saronged, Posh Spiced, Cooled Britannia, look-at-me, what-a-lad, loadsamoney, sex-and-shopping, fame-schooled, daytime

TV, over-coiffed twerp did not, of course, mean any harm (*Daily Telegraph* editorial, 2 July 1998).

This editorial both contained themes that featured in all the national newspapers, and also some references specific to the *Daily Telegraph*'s editorial perspective. The common themes revolved around the effects of commercialisation and celebrity on an individual's self-discipline. The *Daily Telegraph* took the opportunity to cite a range of other manifestations which, for this newspaper, also represented a decline in national standards. In the game against Argentina Beckham, through a display of temperament more stereotypically associated with Latin players, had failed to live up to these 'standards', which were reinforced through representing Beckham as a national disgrace.

Englishness is also constructed through making a distinction between, on the one hand, the nation brought together through support for the national team and, on the other, soccer hooligans. The *Sun*'s blanket coverage on the day of England's opening afternoon game at France '98 is typical of the first. The front page is dominated by a photo of the then BBC1 anchorman Des Lynam, with an associated story backing the *Sun*'s campaign for workers to be allowed time off to watch the match. On page 3 there is a story anticipating deserted workplaces and roads, as the nation communes around its television sets:

ENGLAND IS CLOSED DOWN FOR THE BIG GAME
The nation will virtually shut down this afternoon as millions tune in to cheer England's world Cup heroes on the telly. . . Meanwhile, bosses. . . fear a huge surge of 'sicknote supporters' – with football loving staff phoning at the last moment to get the day off. (*Sun*, 15 June 1998)

Helpfully, the centre page carried an exemplary World Cup sicknote which readers could cut out and present to their bosses. Thus the *Sun* invokes a nation unified around its support for the England soccer team, made possible by the BBC, personified by its popular host. There is nothing exceptional here about the *Sun*'s coverage, it is a way of covering major televised sporting events that can be found across the world.

On pages 4 to 5 of the same issue, the *Sun* ran a double spread headlined 'GOOD, THE BOD AND THE UGLY'. The 'good' referred to '20,000 great supporters', featuring accounts of the extraordinary lengths some fans had gone to in making their way to Marseilles. The 'ugly' referred to '200 drunken louts' who had thrown battles at Tunisia fans and had subsequently been tear-gassed by riot cops. (The 'bod' referred to a photo of ex-page 3 girl Melinda Messenger.) Once again, this coverage is typical of much UK press coverage in making a firm and distinction between right and wrong ways of supporting England: between the vast majority of ordinary fans and the tiny minority of deviant hooligans.

Another distinction that was drawn was between the players and the hooligans. The next day, after England had beaten Tunisia 2–0, the *Sun* (16 June 1998) ran on its cover around a juxtaposition of a photo of Alan Shearer with a photo of one of the 'thugs':

HEROES AND VILLAINS OF ENGLISH FOOTBALL
TWO: Goal-scoring Shearer who led us to first World Cup victory.
NIL: Tattooed thug . . .who led riot that shamed us all.

The juxtaposition of the photographs – in which both men are bare-chested — invites the reader to make a clear comparison between the lean, fit Shearer, and the flabby, tattooed thug; the distinction between national hero and national villain is inscribed in the contrasting physiques.

It should be noted that in much of the coverage of these events over the following days the newspapers attempted to identify the men who had featured in the photographs of the events in Marseilles. For example, the *Daily Express* (16 June 1998) ran a front page, which, below photos of the individuals concerned, asked:

What turns a father of three, a serving soldier and an antiques dealer into thugs who shame our nation?

Despite the implication that soccer hooligans are ordinary people, this kind of coverage doesn't fundamentally deviate from the distinction between ordinary fans and deviant hooligans.

To sum up, the dominant representation of English national identity through media coverage of sport is one that contrasts English national identity with other national identities, and is characterised by a nostalgic discourse comparing the sporting performance of its current team with an imagined golden age. This comparison is based on the extent to which current players exemplify traditional English values. It also distinguishes acceptable and unacceptable ways of supporting the nation.

This dominant representation of English national identity is based on exclusion. For example, according to Carrington (1998: 118), during Euro '96:

> The fact that the majority of the black population living in England had either a large degree of ambivalence towards England or openly supported "anyone but England" underscores the points being made that the form of national identity produced failed to be inclusive and actually alienated large sections of the nation.

And it is safe to assume that the black population were not the only television viewers and newspapers readers alienated by much English coverage of international soccer competitions.

The representation of Englishness through the media coverage of England's sporting teams is obviously gendered. Hobsbawm once remarked about soccer: 'the imagined community of millions seems more real as a team of eleven named people' (1990: 143). But one hardly needs to point out that the eleven named people are men. No women's sports team has got anywhere close to representing the nation in the way that the England men's soccer, cricket and rugby teams have. Only perhaps women competing in the individual events, like Denise Lewis winning the heptathlon at the Sydney Olympics, come close (and in this case she was representing Britain). In the English tabloid newspaper coverage of international soccer competitions the most visible role that women play is as glamour models.

Further, national identity comes into conflict with diasporic identity. Diasporic identity signifies a form of belonging that is fundamentally different from national identity, and arises from the widespread dispersal of populations (diaspora), usually as the result of forced migration. (The dispersal of the Jews is usually cited as the primary example.) Gilroy (2000: 123) sees the idea of diaspora as a rejection of

> the popular image of natural nations spontaneously endowed with self-consciousness . . . As an alternative to the metaphysics of 'race', nation and bounded culture coded into the body, diaspora is a concept that problematises the cultural and historical mechanics of belonging. It disrupts the fundamental power of territory to determine identity by breaking the simple sequence of explanatory links between place, location and consciousness.

Hence diaspora are a problem for nation-states. Again according to Gilroy (2000: 124):

> Consciousness of diasporic affiliation stands opposed to the distinctively modern structures and modes of power orchestrated by the institutional complexity of nation-states. Diasporic identification exists outside of and sometimes in opposition to the political forms and codes of modern citizenship. The nation-state has regularly been presented as the institutional means to terminate diaspora dispersal. At the one end of the communicative circuit this is to be accomplished by the assimilation of those out of place. At the other, a similar outcome is realised through the prospect of their return to a place of origin.

An illustration of the unease caused in nation-states by diaspora can be illustrated in relation to developments regarding cricket in the UK. An example regularly cited in relation to issues around 'race' and sport is the 'Tebbit test'. In 1990, at a time when the Conservative Party was still in power, chairman Norman Tebbit questioned the claims to British citizenship of Asian or black Britons who support other nations at cricket. The 1999 Cricket World Cup based in England was promoted as a 'carnival of cricket'. But whereas white English fans watched passively, what distinguished the competition were scenes of active and visible support demonstrated by second or third-generation British Asians, supporting India or

Pakistan rather than England. Contrary to Tebbit's view, for a British Asian to support India or Pakistan at cricket is not a denial of Britishness but rather an identification with a more inclusive notion of national identity than the one represented by English cricket (Maguire, 1993b: 298–9). As McDonald and Ugra have argued, 'the culture of "English" cricket ... can ... lead to a culture of racial exclusion, racial stereotyping, and to racial abuse of black and Asian players' (1999: 178–9). Diasporic identification through cricket problematises the assumption that the construction of dominant national identities through the sports media of nation-states is inclusive, homogeneous or uncontested. (For a discussion of race, nation and diasporic Indian identity relating to World Series cricket, see also Madan, 2000.)

Finally, the question of the relationship between media sport and identity in the UK raises important issues around the different constructions of national identity in respects of nation-states and 'stateless nations'. Modern sport institutions have helped to construct a separate sense of national cultural identity in Wales, Scotland and Ireland. For example, since 1904, FIFA has treated England, Scotland, Wales and Northern Ireland as separate nations (Duke and Crolley, 1996). There has been substantial research on the role of media coverage of sport in general, and particularly soccer, in the construction of Scottish identity (see for example, Blain and Boyle, 1994; Boyle and Haynes, 1996). There has been much less on Wales, where rugby union is often projected as the symbol of national identity, capable of transcending regional, class and linguistic differences. In the context of recent political devolution and economic regeneration, a wide range of public institutions and commercial organisations have used rugby to market Welsh sport, tourism and business. Examples of how media institutions attempt to reinforce a sense of identification with the nation can be seen in promos for rugby union coverage in Wales. During the opening ceremony for the 1999 Rugby World Cup tournament held in Cardiff, the Welsh language broadcaster S4C ran a promo for its magazine programme, *Y Clwb Rygbi*, shown during the break in coverage transmitted by the regional ITV franchise, HTV

Wales. Over a montage of images of the valleys, quarries, working men, men and boys of various ages playing rugby, a deep male voice proclaims:

> To know the heart and mind of Wales is to know rugby. It is everything. It is inherent in the people. It is built into the psyche. It's about belonging. It's not a phenomenon. It's an everyday matter. It's not about fashion, football or hampers in car parks. It's about going the extra distance. It's about the blood that pumps in the heart. It's about being what you want to be. Live it, love it.

The appeal of this message is understandable, based as it is around an assertion of working-class Welsh identity opposed to English middle-class identity. (The targets of the message are intellectuals, fickle fans who have turned to soccer, posh fans who eat picnics in the car park at Twickenham, home of English rugby). The message seems to be: you don't like rugby, you're not really Welsh. In April 1999 BBC Wales ran a promo for its coverage of Wales v. England in the Five Nations championships featuring a song by Kelly Jones of pop group the Stereophonics, which has the chorus 'As long as we beat the English, we don't care'. Some indication of the lived, historical roots of this aspect of Welsh rugby culture can be found in the following quote from Phil Bennett, then Welsh rugby union captain, in motivating his players before a game against England in 1977:

> These English you're just going to meet have taken our coal, our water, our steel: they buy our houses and live in them a fortnight a year... Down the centuries these English have exploited and pillaged us – and we're playing them this afternoon boys. (*Guardian*, 2 February 1993; cited in Maguire, 1994: 411–12)

And if media institutions in Wales, like BBC Wales or the Welsh language broadcaster S4C, or newspapers such as the *Western Mail* or *Wales on Sunday*, play a major role in reinforcing the construction of Welsh national identity in opposition to Englishness, then it could also be said that much of the London-based 'British' media also play a role through continuing to ignore, patronise, insult or stereotype Wales or Welsh people.

Nevertheless, the use of rugby as a cultural unifier is not without its problems in projecting a modern and inclusive image of Wales. Rugby first played a key role in the formation of modern Welsh identity during the rapid industrialisation of South Wales between 1890 and 1914. What this meant, Andrews argues, was that the 'cultural masculinisation of the modern nation reflected and reinforced the marginal status of the female population' (1996b: 52). As a consequence, the image of Welsh identity projected through rugby tends to be male-oriented and nostalgic, and can easily reinforce negative stereotypes of Welsh identity. Evans, Davies and Bass (1999: 141) offer a useful critique of the idea that rugby union is the defining symbol of Welsh national identity:

> At a time when Wales seeks and needs to remake itself, facing the forces of globalisation, nationalism and the changing socio-environmental requirements of a post-modern age, this narrow cultural specialisation, the hegemony of 'the male game', the social relations it reflects and reproduces, the failure to both recognise and nurture other cultural forms and the voices they represent, may be profoundly damaging not only to the development of more robust and liberal forms of citizenship but to the literal and metaphorical health of the nation-state.

Conclusion

This chapter started by suggesting that it is very difficult to provide a general theory of the specific ways in which media sport constructs national identity across different nations. The examples discussed here have been very limited – a satisfactory analysis of the role of the media in the construction of national identity needs in-depth study (see Gruneau and Whitson, 1993 for an excellent analysis of the role of media in constructing hockey as the national sport of Canada). However, there are some points that arise from this chapter that could provide the starting point for looking at this subject beyond the limited examples discussed here.

Firstly, the ritual dimension of media sport plays a key role in the construction of national identities as 'imagined communities' (Anderson, 1991). At the same time, following Hall (1992), identity formation should be seen as a complex and contradictory process, in which national identity is one form of identity, which intersects with others, such as gender and ethnic identity.

Secondly, representations of national identity in media sport are the site of competing discourses. In analysing the role of media sports coverage in the representation of national identity, we need to examine which sports, stars, styles of play, character traits, etc. are represented as in some way more symbolic of a particular national identity than others, and explore why. The brief discussion of media sport in the US and the UK suggests that dominant discourses of national identity are inextricably interrelated with hegemonic definitions of gender and 'race' (see Chapters 4 and 5).

Thirdly, while it is possible to recognise dominant national identities which coincide with nation-states, there is also resistance to these national identities, particularly in the form of diasporic identities. Finally, the existence of 'stateless nations' within nation-states further represents a challenge to the hegemony of dominant national identities. However, as illustrated in the brief discussion of media promotion of Welsh identities through rugby union, the contribution that media sport makes to the construction of national identities in stateless nations is as problematic and as likely to be implicated with hegemonic discourses of gender and 'race' as that of the larger nation-state.

|5|

Media, sport and the politics of identity 1: Race

In this and the following chapter, a key argument will be that sport has played a fundamental role in the reproduction of unequal power relations. The politics of race and the politics of gender should not be conflated, but in relation to sport there are important similarities in the way in which nature is invoked to legitimise different types of representation. Research in sports sociology and media studies since the 1970s has generally concluded that media sport has played a major role in reinforcing regressive stereotypes, particularly through conservative ideologies around 'natural' difference. Such stereotypes play a key role in legitimising the institutional structures that continue to reproduce racism and sexism in sport.

At the same time, there have been significant changes over the last thirty years, which must have some implications for the ways in which media sport functions in this respect. On the one hand, the politics of the 'new social movements' – anti-racism and feminism – have had substantial effects in identifying and challenging discrimination, and formulating equal rights legislation that has had its implications in terms of sports participation. On the other hand, at least in the more affluent parts of the world, increasing commodification has had important but massive and contradictory effects on the ways in which women and black people are both represented *in the sports media* and targeted *as consumers of media sport* or related products, epitomised perhaps, by the advertisements and marketing strategies pursued by Nike.

The following two chapters propose that changes in both sport and the media documented throughout the book have begun to render problematic the argument that media sport coverage of women or black people is notable primarily for the extent of under-representation or stereotyping. It is suggested that theories of identity which emphasise its contingency and complexity are more useful tools of analysis, given the diversity and increased proliferation of media representations of gender and race in sport.

Biological racism

In order to address issues around 'race' and sport, we firstly need to demolish a myth that enjoys remarkable resilience in this area – the myth that differences between the performances of white and black athletes at particular sport can be explained in terms of biologically determined racial characteristics. According to Donald and Rattansi, in a reader on race and education (1992: 1):

> In genetic terms, the physical or biological differences between groups defined as 'races' have been shown to be trivial. No persuasive empirical case has been made for ascribing common psychological, intellectual or moral capacities or characteristics to individuals on the basis of skin colour or physiognomy.

Similarly, as a leading US sports sociology textbook so effectively explains, attempts by scientists in Europe and then North America since the 1700s to develop a 'biological classification system that objectively divides humans into distinct racial groups' have failed utterly (Coakley, 1998: 250). Whereas humans are endlessly differentiated in terms of skin colour, hair form, body shape, these differences do not correspond to a group of simple biological types. It is worth repeating a quote from Kenneth Kidd, one of the leading biologists and geneticists cited by Coakley (1998: 221):

> The DNA data support the concept that you can't draw boundaries between races. Genetically, I am more similar to someone

from China or the Amazon Basin than two Africans living in the same village are to each other. This substantiates the point that there is no such thing biologically as race.

This bears repetition, because although the idea that there is a biological or genetic basis for racial classification has effectively been abandoned by respectable science, this idea has remarkable resilience in media discourse about sport, either explicitly in debates over black success or failure in particular sports, or implicitly in terms of the ways in which black athletes are stereotypically represented.

It is true that black sports stars are more successful in some sports whilst being almost absent in others. Examples of the former include athletics and basketball, where 80 per cent of players in the NBA could be described as African-American (Wilson, 1997: 177). A traditional explanation for this very visible imbalance is to seek a biological basis for why black athletes are better suited for certain sports rather than others, an explanation which neatly does away with having to engage with sociocultural issues such as the extent of discrimination in particular sports organisations. Recently there has been a new twist on this explanation – that scientific arguments are being suppressed by a 'politically correct' liberal establishment. For example, in 1999 television journalist Jon Entine published a book called *Taboo: Why Black Athletes Dominate Sport and Why We're Afraid to Talk About It*, which generated a lot of media coverage even in liberal newspapers (e.g.'Genetics "the key to black success"', *Observer*, 23 January 2000). The Australian press previewed a 100m race between Linford Christie and Matt Shirvington in 1999 as a battle between white and black ('Can white beat black?' *Observer*, 28 March 1999). The problem is that the attribution of fundamental characteristics based on genetic difference, even if it appears to be based on appreciative acknowledgement of the performance of black athletes, opens up the whole issue of how certain attributes can be ascribed to genetic difference. Here sport can be used to provide the legitimisation for biological racism in general.

One of the areas that Entine uses for 'proof' is the success of Kenyan long-distance runners. Hoberman, himself criticised for his own fascination with this issue (Review symposium, 1998b; Shropshire and Smith, 1998), had already addressed this question (Hoberman, 1997: 240):

> It is possible that there is a population of West African origin that is endowed with an unusual proportion of fast-twitch muscle fibres, and it is somewhat more likely that there are East Africans whose resistance to fatigue, for both genetic and cultural reasons, exceeds that of other racial groups. But these hypotheses are not even close to scientific confirmation. . .

Explanations that seek to locate the success of black athletes in particular sports in 'scientific' classifications of biological difference are arguably more prevalent in the sports media than they are in respectable science. It bears repeating: there is no biological or genetic basis for racial classification. Instead, convincing cultural and social explanations could be put forward to explain the difference in the performance of black and white athletes in certain sports. According to Davis (1990: 185):

> The preoccupation with the question of whether there are racially linked genetic traits that can explain athletic success is racist. The preoccupation is racist because it is founded on and naturalizes the notion that racial categories are fixed and unambiguous biological realities, thus obscuring the political interests underlying the process of racial formation.

However, simply arguing that there is no foundation for the biological explanations of race that have been reproduced in relation to sport does not get rid of the problem. As Donald and Rattansi (1992: 1) argue:

> It is all too clear that racism still remains a widespread, and possibly intensifying, fact of many people's lives. Reiterating that 'there's no such thing as "race"' offers only the frail reassurance that there shouldn't be a problem. It cannot deal with the problems that do exist, because it fails to see them for what they are . . . The issue is not how natural differences determine and justify

group definitions and interactions, but how racial logics and racial frames of reference are articulated and deployed, and with what consequences.

Research in the UK, USA and Western Europe indicates that there is a problem of racism in sport, as in society more generally. There is still an under-representation of black and Asian people in many sports, as there is in higher levels of sports-related occupation, for example, sports administration, coaching, management and sports journalism. And at the level of grass-roots participation and specta-torship in some sports there is evidence that black and Asian people are dissuaded from participation by verbal abuse and the threat of violence. The concept of race might have been dismissed as having no biological or genetic basis, but racism is experienced as only too real by many black or Asian people in and outside sport.

Race as a 'floating signifier'

If the notion of a biological or genetic basis for race has been dis-missed, then 'race' must be a cultural or social construction. A num-ber of commentators have identified a transformation in the discourse of race since the late 1960s, when black activism and anti-racist politics became prominent.

Crudely, what characterises this transformation is a shift from explicit references to fundamental biological difference to a more implicit common-sense racism, based on accepted *essentialist* notions of environmental or cultural difference. These shifts have been described in different terms, which all appear to refer to the same phenomenon.

Hall has made an important distinction between *overt* and *infer-ential* racism in the media. His term overt racism refers to:

those many occasions when open and favourable coverage is given to arguments, positions and spokespersons who are in the business of elaborating an openly racist argument or advancing a racist policy or view ... (Hall, 1990: 12–13)

Hall argued that overt racism could be most clearly identified in the British newspaper press of the early 1980s, which he argued had become 'openly partisan to extremist right-wing arguments' (1990: 13). By contrast, inferential racism refers to

> those apparently naturalised representations of events and situations relating to race, whether 'factual' or 'fictional', which have racist premises and propositions inscribed in them as a set of *unquestioned assumptions*. These enable racist statements to be formulated without ever bringing into awareness the racist predicates on which the statements are grounded . . . inferential racism is more widespread – and in many ways, more insidious [than overt racism], because it is largely *invisible* even to those who formulate the world in its terms. (Hall, 1990: 13)

An example of 'inferential racism' for Hall is the type of programme that deals with a 'race relations' problem, probably made with the best of intentions, but which is 'predicated on the unstated and unrecognised assumption that *blacks* are the *source of the problem*' (1990: 13).

The media examples that Hall uses are perhaps not the most relevant to the discussion of the sports media. But the point is that racism in the media does not need to take overt or negative forms to be racism – apparently celebratory media representations can be racist if they are predicated on racist assumptions. (For an extended discussion of racism in sports reporting which draws on Hall's distinction, see Tudor, 1998.)

The 'floating racial signifier' is a concept formulated by Stuart Hall in the context of his theoretical work on identities and race in the late 1980s and early 1990s (see the Media Education Foundation video, *Race: the Floating Signifier*, 1996). The floating racial signifier, as it suggests, indicates that the meanings of race are not *fixed* – what the same racial signifier means changes at any given moment in time. According to Andrews, Michael Jordan's 'racial identity is not stable, essential or consistent; it is dynamic, complex and contradictory' (1996c: 126). In analysing the representation of black athletes in media and sport, as there are no essential meanings but only historically specific ones, it is important to locate these within the specific historical political, economic and social context in which media representations are produced, circulated and consumed. The concept of the floating racial signifier thus problematises the notion of stereotype, which tends to essentialise and reduce the semantic complexities of images of race in media sport.

The commodification of black sport

As discussed in Chapter 3, the economics of sport has undergone a fundamental 'post-industrial' transformation, characterised by a greater emphasis on the economic value of the image. The sports shoe industry, and Nike in particular, has been at the forefront in using advertisements, endorsements and sponsorship to differentiate products which are in essence very similar. In aggressively pursuing certain marketing strategies, Nike has played a major role in deliberately constructing many of the images associated with sport. Race has been central to Nike's advertisements, in one way or another, and in discussing recent representations of race associated with media sport it would be impossible to underestimate their role.

McKay (1995) contrasts two different images of black protest as evidence of the increasing commodification of that protest. At the 1968 Mexico Olympics Tommie Smith and John Carlos achieved gold/bronze medals in 200m. According to McKay (1995: 191), 'both had removed shoes and rolled up their sweatpants as a symbol of black Americans' poverty.' During the US anthem they gave the Black Power salute whilst bowing their heads. The photograph has become an iconic image. As a result of this protest they were stripped of medals, disqualified by the IOC, and sent home by the US team. McKay notes how the photo has been used in a subsequent advertisement for Puma Suedes, the shoes actually removed by Smith and Carlos, in a fashion and music magazine aimed at young, affluent black readers. The political gesture had become part of a commodified 'legacy of cool' (1995: 192).

McKay compares this with a protest at the Barcelona Olympics in

1992 by the US basketball team. Sportswear firm Reebok was the official sponsor of the Olympics and supplied warm-up suits to the US team. Michael Jordan and Charles Barkley wrapped themselves in the US-flag to obscure the Reebok logos. Barkley explained, 'Us Nike guys are loyal to Nike because they pay us a lot of money. I have two million reasons not to wear Reebok' (McKay, 1995: 199). Thus whereas in 1968 a political protest by black athletes was staged to express solidarity with black people in the US, in 1992 a protest by black sports stars was one about company loyalty.

How to interpret this development? McKay situates it in the context of the growth of enlightened racism. Cashmore sees it as part of the growth of a black cultural industry: 'Thirty years ago, whites were taught to fear difference ... today ... whites not only appreciate black culture: they buy it' (Cashmore, 1997: 1). This has meant that 'black culture has been converted into a commodity ... blacks have been permitted to excel in entertainment only on the condition that they conform to whites' images of blacks' (Cashmore, 1997: 1). Hence these developments can be interpreted as on the one hand using sport to fix black culture as something essentially different and desirable, through the processes of commodification. These commodified images fit with traditional stereotypes around black people as entertainers, attributed to black people being better at expressive than at intellectual activities, being better at activities of the body than of the mind.

'Role models' and 'bad boys'

This discussion will draw on the argument that a key discursive strategy in the representation of black sports stars is the distinction that is made, according to Wenner, between 'good blacks' and 'bad blacks' (Wenner 1995; see also Wilson, 1997). In white European and North American culture this dichotomous representation of the racialised 'other' has a history going back to at least the beginning of the eighteenth century, expressed in the distinction between the 'noble savage' and the uncivilised barbarian. However, as noted above, this representation is always under the process of transformation: representations of black athletes take on specific meanings related to the historical and cultural context through which these representations are produced and consumed. Further, to reiterate the theme that runs through this section, the distinction that is made is based on a relational difference and is unstable. One moment a sports celebrity is a role model, the next a 'bad boy' and the ideological significance of this is related to how easily the meanings attached to a particular sports celebrity can shift from one to the other. The argument of this section will be that Wenner's distinction between 'good blacks' and 'bad blacks' in sport can be usefully expressed through debates over 'role models' and 'bad boys' (and I use this term advisedly, see below).

First, role models. Following McKay (1995), I would propose that Jhally and Lewis' notion of 'enlightened racism' as a means of understanding the significance of the *Cosby Show* is very useful in understanding the 'role model' in sport. In this major audience study of the success of the *Cosby Show*, which investigated white and black audiences, the authors conclude that:

> Among white people, the admission of black characters to television's upwardly mobile world gives credence to the idea that racial divisions, whether perpetuated by class barriers or by racism, do not exist . . . The Cosby-Huxtable persona tells viewers that, as one respondent put it, 'There really is room in the United States for minorities to get ahead, without affirmative action.' (Jhally and Lewis, 1992: 135)

At the same time, 'after suffering years of negative media stereotyping, most black viewers were delighted by a show that portrayed African Americans as intelligent, sensitive and successful' (Jhally and Lewis, 1992: 138).

The starting point for this discussion is that it is the specific context of conservative political reaction to affirmative action that likewise provides the context for media representations of black sports stars in the United States in the 1990s and beyond. A superficially more enlightened form of racism has developed which is based on the belief that whereas in the past legislation was required to establish basic equal rights, there is now no longer any need for affirmative measures to promote black employment or political representation. According to this view, the fictional character of Cliff Huxtable both demonstrates that it is possible for a black person to succeed in a professional role through hard work. And yet

> most white people know that in the world at large, black people achieve less material success, on the whole, than white people. They know that black people are disproportionately likely to live in poor neighbourhoods and drop out of school ... If we are blind to the roots of racial equality embedded in our society's class structure, then there *is* only one way to reconcile this paradoxical state of affairs. If white people are disproportionately successful, then they must be disproportionately smarter or more willing to work hard. The face of Cliff Huxtable begins to fade into the more sinister and threatening face of Willie Horton [the convicted murderer whose negative image was central to advertisements for Bush's republican presidential campaign in 1988]. (Jhally and Lewis, 1992: 136)

The explanation for black underachievement does not have to be sought in biology or genetics. Jhally and Lewis argue that conservative policymakers are increasingly influential on US governments through the 'culture of poverty thesis': that the 'problems of the ghetto underclass originate from the culture of that class itself and that the solution is to change their values' (Jhally and Lewis, 1992: 137).

The Cosby Show plays a role in reinforcing this perception through its representation of a prosperous black family who appear to have succeeded precisely because they have 'changed their values'. The meaning of Cosby/Huxtable is based on the extent to which the character is distanced from more familiar images associated with black people in the media.

I propose here that the significance of black role models in sport functions in the same way as Cosby/Huxtable. Two of the most successful sports stars, particularly in terms of endorsement, have been ones whose 'role model' status has been particularly important. On the one hand, they have been represented as if their racial identity has no significance – i.e. these types of representations are 'colour-blind', with less racial coding. Yet their significance lies precisely in relation to other symbols of race. To illustrate this I would like to take two role models, Michael Jordan and Tiger Woods, and contrast these with the ultimate bad black sportsman, Mike Tyson.

Michael Jordan has been one of the most significant sportsmen of the last two decades of the twentieth century (Andrews 1996a, 1996c; Andrews *et al.*, 1996; Cole, 1996; Denzin, 1996; Jackson and Andrews, 1999b; Kellner, 1996). He is the archetypal modern sports star, able to generate income not just through salaries but also through endorsements. According to *Forbes' Magazine*'s 1998 rich list, Jordan was the top-earning sportsman at $69m – $38m more than the runner-up Michael Schumacher. His career coincided with the employment of aggressive commercial strategies by the NBA from the 1980s predominantly based on the commodification of black sporting personalities. For much of Jordan's career he has been represented in the media as a positive role model, in opposition to the often negative linking of basketball to a black urban ghetto culture. When the owner of the Chicago Bulls, Jerry Reinsdorf, said 'Is Michael Jordan black? . . . Michael has no colour', he was expressing a commonly held white perception of Jordan. However, during a series of controversies in 1991 and 1992, including accusations of a gambling addiction, Jordan was for a time represented in terms of racial otherness, as the archetypal black male (Andrews, 1996c: 125, 142–6).

Other critical analyses have discussed how the representation of black athletes in white-dominated media oscillates between the images of the 'role model' and racial other: for example, in the cases of Ben Johnson (Jackson, 1998) and 'Magic' Johnson (Cole and Denny, 1995; King, 1993; Rowe, 1994). As Jackson and Meier have shown, in Canadian sports media coverage, 'Ben Johnson continues to haunt and overshadow the achievements' of the Jamaican-Canadian sprinter Donovan Bailey (1999: 185).

Tiger Woods is the archetypal example of how racial identities cannot be easily fixed. He has referred to himself as 'Cablinasian'

(*Ca*ucasian, *B*lack, *In*dian, *Asian*), or more specifically 'one-fourth Thai, one-fourth Chinese, one-fourth African-American, one-eighth Native American, and one-eighth white European' (Coakley, 1998: 251). This mixed background means that in different media discourses different aspects of his identities are projected onto him: sometimes black, sometimes Asian. This, combined with Woods' ability to demolish opponents on the golf course, explains why he has become the most highly paid individual sports star, taking over from Michael Jordan. Woods was sponsored by Nike from 1996 to $40m, and in September 2000 he was reported to have signed a five-year $100m contract extension, the most lucrative endorsement contract ever ('Woods hits the $100m jackpot', *Guardian*, 16 September 2000). Here again, complexity characterises the representation of this black/Asian sportsman in the American media. On the one hand, Woods is 'America's new son', 'coded as a multicultural sign of colour blindness' (Cole and Andrews, 2000: 120; see also Polunbaum and Wieting, 1999), distinct from the black players of the NBA, who stand for black urban masculinity. On the other hand, the role of Nike tends to construct continuities with their previously sponsored black athletes. Tiger Woods' success in the previously white-dominated sport of golf becomes a sign that anyone can make it in America whatever their ethnic background – whilst at the same time it is shorn of the connotations that go with the 'inner-city' black culture associated with the NBA.

Mike Tyson cuts a very different figure. Unlike Michael Jordan, he does not feature as a role model. Instead he fits into the white stereotype of the ghetto animal. In his analysis of the February 1992 newspaper coverage of the trial of Mike Tyson for the rape of Desiree Washington, Lule argues that Tyson was represented as 'either a crude, sex-obsessed, violent savage who could barely control his animal instincts or he was a victim of terrible social circumstances, almost saved from the streets by a kindly overseer [veteran trainer and 'surrogate father' Cus d'Amato], but who finally faltered and fell to the connivance of others' (1995: 181; see also Sloop, 1997). This type of representation also ran through a range of biographical depictions, such as the HBO TV movie *Tyson* (1995).

Tyson himself contributes to the representation of himself as both an animal and as a helpless victim of tragic circumstances. Responding at a press conference to a question about his use of anti-depressants, he explained:

> I'm on the Zoloft to keeping me from killing y'all. It has really messed me up, and I don't want to be taking it, but they are concerned about the fact that I am a violent person, almost an animal. And they only want me to be an animal in the ring . . . I'm a street person. I never wanted to be a street person; I don't even like them. But that's how my life has turned out. I've had a lot of tragedy ('Tyson rages at "freak show" jibe', *Guardian*, 16 September 2000).

Tyson is such an important figure in sport because of the particular significance that he has. As was noted in Chapter 1, the formation of modern sport is about the exercise of violence, but the exercise of a disciplined, controlled, regulated violence that minimises the risk of serious injury or death to one of the participants. In his later career, Tyson has regularly transgressed these limits. In June 1997 he was banned by the Nevada commission for biting off part of Evander Holyfield's ear. At a bout in Glasgow in June 2000 he continued punching his opponent Lou Savarese after the fight was over and floored the referee. At a press conference he exceeded the boundaries of acceptable trash-talking by promising potential opponent Lennox Lewis: 'I am going to rip your heart out. I want to eat your children' (Mee, 2000). For many, Tyson's later career has become a circus, a succession of short bouts against poor opponents in countries where he is fighting purely to maximise his income before the end of his career. Lewis's manager, Frank Maloney, summarised the typical commentator's take on Tyson:

> What can you expect with Mike Tyson in the ring? It is all a game. It is not boxing, it is a carnival. Boxing goes out of the window when Mike Tyson is around. It is not a sport, it is like going to the circus. ('Maloney laughs at bully-boy Tyson', www.sky.com 26 June 2000)

A common theme of media coverage of Tyson is that he is bringing the sport of boxing into disrepute, a theme perhaps reinforced by his participation in WWF's *Wrestlemania XIV*.

So while many black sportsmen are represented through the distinction between 'role model' (Jordan) and 'bad boy' (Tyson), others have challenged this stereotyping in the media. A key figure here is the basketball player Charles Barkley. Barkley has been used in Nike's advertisements in ways which appear to conflict. On the one hand, he appeared in a controversial advertisement that challenged the idea that sports stars should act as moral 'role models'. In this, speaking directly and frankly to camera, Barkley declaims:

> I am not a role model.
> I am not paid to be a role model.
> I am paid to wreak havoc on the basketball court.
> Parents should be role models.
> Just because I can dunk a basketball
> Doesn't mean I should raise your kids.

According to Goldman and Papson, in whose book this is cited, the advertisement provoked adverse criticism from television and newspapers as well as hostile letters from the public directed at Nike (1998: 85–6). By contrast in March 1994, Barkley participated in a campaign for Nike that had a very assertive moral message: the P. L. A. Y. (Participate in the Lives of American Youth campaign).

When he was playing for the Philadelphia 76ers Charles Barkley used the locker room to criticise the white sports media for ignoring the social and economic deprivation in the black inner-city areas of Philadelphia:

> Just because you give Charles Barkley a lot of money, it doesn't mean I'm going to forget about the people in the ghettos and slums. . . Ya'll don't want me talking about this stuff, but I'm going to voice my opinions, because this stuff's important. Me getting twenty rebounds ain't important. We've got people

homeless on our streets, and the media is crowding around my locker. It's ludicrous.

As a result, he was criticised by the Philadelphia sports media for speaking out on non-sport issues. As was noted in Chapter 2, the institutional structures of sports journalism heavily proscribe what types of issues are discussed: performance, strategies, injuries, and transfers. Barkley transgressed these by daring to speak of issues beyond sport.

It is undeniable that one of the consequences of commodification is to empower black sports stars to some extent. Stars such as Charles Barkley and Dennis Rodman now earn salaries considerably higher than those of the people they deal with, including journalists and coaches. Yet the increasing media representation of black sportsmen contrasts with the lack of black people in media and sports management (Boyd, 1997: 134).

Finally it should be noted that this dual representation of 'role models'/'bad boys' focuses predominantly on sports*men*. Here race cannot be thought of in isolation from gender. The types of resistance and empowerment that Barkley and Rodman could be said to represent is predominantly male resistance and empowerment. This type of rebellion intersects with popular cultural forms based on black urban working-class masculinity: particularly hip-hop (Boyd, 1997). But as Hall (1996: 472) argues:

> Certain ways in which black men continue to live out their counter-identities as black masculinities and replay those fantasies of black masculinities in the theatres of popular culture are, when viewed from along other axes of difference, the very masculine identities that are oppressive to women, that claim visibility for their hardness only at the expense of the vulnerability of black women and the femininisation of gay black men.

Through discussion of 'race' and the sports media it should be apparent that any interpretation that sees media sport representations simply in terms of *either* white stereotypes of black people *or* images of black resistance or empowerment, is far too simplistic. Media representations are much more complex than this, open to a variety of readings from different audiences. And identities are much more complex than this, the ways in which 'race' is lived out as a social identity is inseparable from identities based around gender, nation, class and sexuality.

6

Media, sport and the politics of identity 2: gender

So why does sport matter in terms of gender politics? There are two issues here, inextricably linked and impossible to discuss separately: the ideological role of sport in maintaining unequal power relations between men and women, and the disparity between the resources and the amount of media attention given to male and female sport.

Firstly, the wider ideological role of sport. Sport plays a key role in legitimising particular ideologies around masculinity and femininity that support the domination of women by men. While male domination is being challenged in nearly every other sector of society, there is a whole field of activity where male dominance just seems to be taken for granted. The implications of this range from the exclusion of women from workplace discussions of sporting events, through the ubiquity of sporting metaphors in the language of business and politics, to the legitimisation of male violence.

The link between sport and violence and/or sexual abuse by men against women has become one of the key issues within sports sociology. There is evidence that North American sportsmen are disproportionately more likely to be involved in violent activities (Benedict, 1997; Benedict and Yeager, 1998). Sexual abuse of female athletes by male coaches has been identified as a major problem by researchers (Brackenridge, 1997; Volkwein *et al*, 1997) and by the Women's Sports Foundation. Heywood (2000: 114) proposes that there may be a connection between assumptions about gender difference that underpin coaching practices, and the problem of sexual abuse and harassment.

In at least two ways the media are directly implicated in the link between sport and violence/sexual abuse. Firstly, there are indications that incidents of domestic violence increase during the period when particular sporting events are being broadcast. In 1993 journalist Robert Lipsyte renamed the Super Bowl the Abuse Bowl, although, according to Sabo, Gray and Moore (2000), a preoccupation with televised sports is unlikely to be the sole factor in spouse abuse. Secondly, the media play a role in representing domestic violence involving sportsmen in a particular way. There have been a number of studies of this coverage: on O. J. Simpson (McKay and Smith, 1995; Johnson and Roediger, 1997); Mike Tyson (Lule, 1995; Sloop, 1997); the boxer Sugar Ray Leonard (Messner and Solomon, 1993), and baseball player Wilfredo Cordero and football coach Dan McCarney (McDonald, 1999). These studies tend to demonstrate that the issue of male violence against women is marginalised through individualisation, although, significantly, when the violence is perpetrated by black or Latino men, media reports tend to accentuate and report it as a sign of the 'presumed pathology of an entire race or culture' (McDonald, 1999: 112).

Women's increased success in sport could play a major role in challenging exclusive representations of masculinity as the gender of physical prowess. However, this brings us to the second issue: the inequality between men and women within sport and its related activities. While there has been a significant increase in women's participation in sport since the 1970s, their contribution is still marginalised, particularly in the media. Girls are much less likely to be encouraged to take part in competitive sport in the first instance than boys, and are less likely to be able to make a living from it.

While examining both these issues, particularly with regard to the role of the media, this chapter also considers to what extent processes of globalisation and commodification have transformed political and social issues. It could be argued that the proliferation of media sport has enabled greater visibility for women competitors, the increased targeting of women as consumers of sport, and the use by companies such as Nike of assertive images and language associated with a type of 'popular feminism' (Cole and Hribar, 1995), represent a significant moment in the history of the ideological significance of sport. The last section of the chapter will investigate these claims in more detail.

The reproduction of gender inequalities through sport

Before examining the role of the media in the reproduction of inequalities in sport, it is important to acknowledge that sport organisations have institutionalised inequalities. During the period where modern sports were 'invented', women were effectively excluded. Views on natural biological difference were used to justify the exclusion of women from sport. Late nineteenth-century ideologies of femininity defined women in terms of childbearing, and physical activity was seen as something that was potentially dangerous (Cahn, 1994: 7–30; Cashmore, 1999; Hargreaves, 1994: 43–50). Women were encouraged to participate only in those sports that were seen as less physically demanding. For example, women competed at the Wimbledon tennis championships from 1884.

However, just because women were not socially encouraged to compete at sport did not mean that they didn't compete. Women have long participated in particular sports, but that participation has tended to become 'hidden from history'. In Liverpool in 1919 53,000 spectators watched a soccer game between St Helens Ladies and Dick Kerr's Ladies (Williams and Woodhouse, 1991: 92).

The role of sports organisations has dramatically changed over the last thirty years or so, and they now promote equal opportunities as part of their mission statements. Yet from time to time news emerges about obviously discriminatory practices carried out by sports institutions. FIFA registered sports agent Rachel Anderson was excluded from the Professional Footballers' Association (PFA) dinner on the grounds that it was a male only *social* event. However, it is through such events that agents are able to make contact with players, and Anderson argued that in being excluded from such an event she was discriminated against. The English cricket club responsible for the laws of the game, the Marylebone Cricket Club (MCC), only recently lifted their exclusion on women members, and even now that women have been admitted they are subject to a dress code.

The sports media have tended to marginalise the extent of participation of women in sport. This has important financial and promotional implications.

On the financial side, there is the question of raising revenue. Sports organisations can effectively generate revenue from the media in two different but interrelated ways. The first is the sale of rights, the second is sponsorship revenue that increased visibility in the media can bring. This income is essential to the development of sport. It can offer increased individual rewards (which are crucial in terms of whether players/athletes can turn professional), and can enable improved facilities for sports, to benefit participation in general.

On the promotional side, there is the question of quantity and nature of coverage. If we assume that identification with role models in the media is likely to encourage children to participate, then girls are far less likely to feel encouraged, because they will encounter few role models. The overexposure of sportsmen and underexposure of sportswomen is likely to reinforce the idea that women in sport are unusual. Neither *Forbes Magazine*'s rich list of the 25 richest sports stars in the US in 1998, nor Radio 5 Live's UK rich list of 10, had any women mentioned (*Guardian*, 7 March 2000). Indeed, in the UK only one woman, golfer Laura Davies, would have made it into the top 100 sports money earners ('British women a long way behind on money list', *Guardian*, 11 May 2000).

The manner in which coverage is framed is also significant. Apart from stereotyping of female sports stars (see below), the media help create the impression that female participation is at best slightly odd.

Given the attitude reflected in the media, it is not surprising that women are under-represented in most sports-related activities. In the UK women make up half the students studying sports subjects, but only a third of those employed in the sports and leisure industries, and less than 10 per cent of heads of organisations within this sector ('Jobs for the boys', *Guardian*, 17 September 1998). It has already been noted how few women are sports journalists.

As I have noted in Chapter 3, sport is a major economic activity. Hence it should not be a considered a peripheral social distraction. Discrimination is as significant here as in any other professional or commercial sphere.

The asymmetrical representation of gender in media coverage

In analysing the representation of masculinity and femininity in media sports coverage the key point is that this representation is asymmetrical. There have been a number of sophisticated quantitative studies of the balance of media coverage dedicated to men's and women's sport (see for example, Duncan *et al.*, 1994; Eastman and Billings, 2000). Theoretically, the results of these studies should vary according to whether the period of time under analysis included a big event likely to skew the results(e.g. the Olympic Games); whether the study was on sports coverage in general or whether the study was of a particular event or of a particular sport; whether the study was on newspaper or broadcast coverage; whether the research was conducted in a nation in which particular women's sports have a higher profile than in other nations; and even, how the coverage was quantified, whether in terms of number of stories or column inches for newspapers, or number of stories or clock time for broadcast coverage.

Nevertheless, despite all these possible variations, it seems unarguable that overall coverage of men's sports massively exceeds that of women's sports. Indeed, most of the studies show that, *in general*, coverage of women's sport routinely amounts to less than 10 per cent of the total available. Of course, media coverage of particular events, such as the Olympic Games, can demonstrate a more even, if not equal, balance (Eastman and Billings, 2000). Higgs and Weiller (1994) found that at the 1992 Summer Olympics 44 per cent of US coverage went to women athletes competing in those sports in which both men and women took part. Toohey found that sportswomen accounted for 33 per cent of Australian coverage of the 1996 Olympics (1997), and Tuggle and Owen (1999) concluded that women's sports amounted to between 43 and 57 per cent of US television coverage, with the higher figures relating to coverage of stereotypical women's sport (diving, field hockey, etc.).

But in a way the extra attention on such occasions as the Olympic Games only serves to reinforce the message. The Olympic Games happens every four years (or two if the Winter Olympics is included) and is, by definition, an extraordinary event. If coverage of the Olympic Games is more balanced, this does little to compensate for the routine day-in day-out imbalance in coverage. Even during periods when major women's sporting events take place, the routine balance of coverage does not seem to change (Eastman and Billings, 2000: 209). Through this imbalance in media coverage, sportswomen are, to use Kane and Greendorfer's application of Gerbner's phrase, subject to 'symbolic annihilation' (Gerbner, 1978; Kane and Greendorfer, 1994).

Below I aim to identify a number of hypotheses from the existing literature which need to be tested against specific research data.

The media treatment of men's and women's sport will be affected by stereotypical assumptions about what is 'male-appropriate' and 'female-appropriate'. A common theme running through research on the representation of gender is that the media will focus on different sports according to an ideological distinction between what are seen as male-appropriate and female-appropriate sports. Male-appropriate sports are those in which the desired qualities – power, strength, etc. – happen to coincide with dominant definitions of masculinity. Male-appropriate sports account for the majority of sports represented in the media. Female-appropriate sports are those in which the desired qualities – style, grace etc. – are those stereotypically attributed to femininity. Female-appropriate sports are those that do not include physical contact, and are sports in which participants are more likely to compete as individuals than as teams. So for example, women's rugby union does not get as much coverage as tennis, gymnastics or ice skating. Representations of women participating in sport are more acceptable only when they are more stereotypically feminine and emphasise sexuality. This of course has implications for the types of sports that are likely to be covered.

Women's sports are likely to be subject to gender-marking. Messner, Duncan and Jensen (1993) argue that in their study of television commentary covering men's and women's tennis and basketball, stereotyping identified by previous studies around sexualisation, trivialisation, infantilisation, etc. was not present to any noticeable extent. More pervasive, however, was gender-marking – the marking of women's sport as 'other'. The common practice of referring to 'basketball' when it is played by men but 'women's basketball' when its played by women reinforces the notion that women's sport is unusual, to be marked out as different. The argument can be generalised. Even when the media covers women's sport positively it often does so in a way which heavily signposts its difference. In this way, representation of gender in sport can be said to be asymmetrical.

Images of women will typically be subject to sexualisation. Kane and Greendorfer point to the coverage of Florence Griffith-Joyner at the 1988 and 1992 Olympics as typical of this superficial visibility, arguing that although images of FloJo proliferated, it was because of her glamorous image, her 'multicolored high-fashion outfit', her other persona as fashion model/designer, focusing on her femininity and sexuality rather than her athleticism. By contrast, they argue, Jackie Joyner Kersee – winner of the gold medal in the heptathlon at the same two Olympics – received much less attention due to her less stereotypically feminine appearance. And those who do not match the expected feminine image are represented as unnatural, deviant, etc.

Sportswomen will be infantilised in television commentary. A very simple and obvious illustration is to label sportswomen as 'girls' whereas sportsmen are hardly ever described as 'boys'. Another aspect to this is the use of first names to refer to sportswomen whereas sportsmen are typically referred to by their surnames.

Trivialisation. This refers to the representation of female achievements in sport as less significant than the achievements of their male counterparts, or at least to displaying ambivalence as to their significance. Achievements of sportswomen who feature in the media are more likely to be represented as *personal* victories. It is difficult to envisage sportswomen being held up by the media as being representative of the nation in the way that, for example, male soccer or rugby teams are. This is partly to do with the fact that those women's sports that are visible in the media are more likely to be individual rather than team sports.

Familialisation. The argument here is that there is a tendency in media coverage of women's sport to discuss sports stars in terms of marital status, private lives, personal problems, and – particularly – motherhood, etc. The ideological implications of such a strategy is to locate women in the home, reinforcing traditional public/private sphere boundaries.

Hegemonic masculinity

A key concept that underpins many studies of sport and masculinity is that of 'hegemonic masculinity' (Davis, 1997; Dworkin and Wachs, 1998, 2000; Jansen and Sabo, 1994; Trujillo, 1990, 1995). Hegemonic masculinity is the taken-for-granted, or 'common sense' model of what it is to be male. According to Connell (1995: 76):

'Hegemonic masculinity' is not a fixed character type, always and everywhere the same. It is, rather, the masculinity that occupies the hegemonic position in a given pattern of gender relations, a position always contestable.

Hegemonic masculinity is the 'culturally idealized form of masculine character (in a given historical setting) which may not be the usual form of masculinity at all' (Connell, 1990: 83). 'But the concept is also inherently relational. '"Masculinity" does not exist except in contrast with "femininity"' (Connell, 1995: 68). Through its definition in opposition to femininity, hegemonic masculinity works to legitimise not just the 'subordination of women' and the 'marginalisation of gay men' (Connell, 1990: 94), but also other subordinated masculinities, 'some heterosexual men and boys too are expelled from the circle of legitimacy' (1995: 79). Just as the concept of hegemony was used within cultural studies to avoid reductive and mechanistic formulations of ideology, so here hegemonic masculinity refers to a contested definition, always contested, and in accommodating consent from subordinate groups, often incoherent.

The usefulness of a concept of masculinity is that acknowledges the existence of other definitions of masculinity is particularly felt in relation to race. According to Connell, hegemonic masculinity is equated with the white, middle-class, heterosexual definition. Nevertheless this does not mean that subordinate masculinities do not support hegemonic masculinity. In order to examine how representations in media sport function to reproduce dominant definitions of masculinity, it is essential, not just desirable, to look at issues of race, class and sexuality.

> Because gender is a way of structuring social practice in general, not a special type of practice, it is unavoidably involved with other social structures. It is now common to say that gender 'intersects' – better, interacts – with race and class. We might add that it constantly interacts with nationality or position in the world order ... To understand gender, then, we must constantly go beyond gender. The same applies in reverse. We cannot understand class, race or global inequality without constantly moving towards gender. (Connell, 1995: 75–6)

There is no single, unitary and fixed masculinity, but rather

> different kinds of masculine character within society that stand
> in complex relations of dominance over and subordination to
> each other ... masculinities are constructed through processes
> that are discontinuous and contradictory (and often experi-
> enced as such). (Connell, 1990: 83)

Where does the media sport fit into Connell's theory of gender?
Connell argues that masculinity and femininity are 'gender projects
... processes of configuring practice through time' (1995: 72). He
argues that there are three sites of gender configuration: the individual life course; 'discourse, ideology or culture'; and 'institutions such
as the state, the workplace and the school'. As part of 'discourse, ideology or culture', how masculinity is represented in the sports media
is then only one aspect of how hegemonic masculinities are produced
and reproduced.

Fundamental to Connell's theory is that masculinity and femininity are always defined in relation to each other. So what does
Connell say about femininity? For Connell, gender is asymmetric:
'there is no form of femininity that is hegemonic in the sense that
the dominant form of masculinity is hegemonic among men'
(Connell, 1987: 183). Instead, Connell uses the term 'emphasized
femininity', 'which is defined around compliance with [the global
subordination of women to men] and is oriented to accommodating the interests and desires of men' (Connell, 1987: 183). By
contrast,

> Others are defined centrally by strategies of resistance of forms
> of non-compliance. Others again are defined by complex strate-
> gic combinations of compliance, resistance and co-operation.
> The interplay among them is a major part of the dynamics of the
> change in the gender order as a whole. (Connell, 1987: 183-4)

For Connell, femininity cannot be hegemonic because

> First, the concentration of social power in the hands of men
> leaves limited scope for women to construct instutionalized

power relationships over other women ... Second, the organization of a hegemonic form around dominance over the other sex is absent from the social construction of femininity. Power, authority, aggression, technology are not thematized in femininity at large as they are in masculinity. Equally important, no pressure is set up to negate or subordinate other forms of femininity in the way hegemonic masculinity must negate other masculinities. It is likely therefore that actual femininities in our society are more diverse than actual masculinities. (Connell, 1987: 187)

Davis (1997, Review symposium, 1998b) argues that there is a dominant/normative form of femininity, which corresponds with hegemonic masculinity, even if it doesn't itself result in societal power (Review symposium 1998a: 202).

The key point about hegemonic masculinity is that it is the form of masculinity at any given moment that comes to be *taken for granted*, to be beyond question. When we encounter media images that immediately jump out at us as obvious media images of masculinity, although these have their significance, perhaps we are looking in the wrong place. Such representations are mainly about sportsmen involved in 'excessive' violence, either on or off the field. It is the images of sportsmen that we consume daily but don't look at twice which are the most significant in terms of the reproduction of definitions of hegemonic masculinity.

Newspaper sport supplements and television schedules are completely dominated by photographs and footage of sportsmen taking part in routine action. Through this normal everyday coverage, readers and viewers are encouraged to equate the controlled aggression central to sport with masculinity. When masculinity is made explicit it is likely to be through some form of transgression, either on or off the sports field.

An example of the first: French soccer player Eric Cantona (playing for Manchester United) kicked, kung-fu style, a member of the crowd who was subjecting him to xenophobic abuse after he was sent off during a match against Crystal Palace in January 1995. The

UK media condemned his actions, in some cases, as an inevitable outcome of his 'gallic temperament'. Thus this reporting 'produced a set of essentialist discourses that conflated narratives of race and ethnicity with deviant or criminal behaviour' (Boyle and Haynes, 2000: 109). For an example of the second, see the discussion of media coverage of Mike Tyson's violent behaviour in Chapter 5 (pp. 118–20).

The point being stressed in both these cases is that the sports media tend to condemn the actions of these sportsmen. In neither case is their behaviour held up as a model of masculinity to be emulated. My argument is that hegemonic masculinity defines itself particularly against such images of excessive or violent masculinity.

Hegemonic masculinity, being by definition taken for granted, is only really brought to light in cases such as the one above. What, then, about the case of the sportsman whose media persona deliberately draws attention to conventional gender roles by continually transgressing them? Throughout the 1990s the basketball player Dennis Rodman dyed his hair in shocking colours, had multiple tattoos and piercings, and played with homoerotic imagery. In his autobiography *Bad as I Wanna Be*, Rodman claimed, 'I've become totally confident about being who I am. I can go out to a salon and have my nails painted pink, and then go out and play in the NBA, on national television, with pink nails' (Rodman and Keown, 1997: 209). He has also worn make-up and dressed in a wedding gown for an MTV documentary. Unsurprisingly, all this has made Rodman the subject of several tactical analyses. Most of these have concluded that his crossdressing is mainly a device to assert his 'bad' persona, which limits its potential for problematising conventional roles of gender and sexuality (Boyd, 1997; Dunbar, 2000; LaFrance and Rail, 2001).

Sportswomen, post-feminism and the commodification of sport

In the late 1990s Mattel launched the WNBA Barbie range, endorsed by WNBA star Rebecca Lobo. Barbie and her friends Christie, Kira and Teresa came with their own WNBA uniforms, warm-up jackets, socks, shoes, kneepads and accessories such as a hairbrush. WNBA Barbie also had a special arm, which could shoot baskets. What, if anything, does the launch of sport-related Barbies tell us about how the media now represents women's sport?

A common argument is that recent changes in sport and the media mean that media sport plays a much more 'progressive' role in terms of furthering gender equality. Cole (2000b) has identified a number of developments in the USA from 1996 onwards that have led mainstream media to proclaim that women have made major gains in sport: the 1996 Atlanta Olympics (labelled by NBC the 'Games of the Woman' – particularly for track and field athletics and gymnastics); the launch of the WNBA (Banet-Weiser, 1999; McDonald, 2000); and the women's soccer World Cup. According to this frame, the genesis of this development was the enactment of Title IX of the civil rights legislation in 1972, which formed part of the education amendments. Title IX stated that

> No person in the United States shall, on the basis of sex, be excluded from participation in, be denied the benefits of, or be subjected to discrimination under any education program or activity receiving federal financial assistance.

What this meant effectively was that no publicly funded school or college could provide funds for any sport that would benefit only one gender. Title IX has led to a massive increase in participation by girls and women. Whatever criticisms can be made about the extent to which this legislation has been successfully *implemented* (Boutilier and SanGiovanni, 1994), the measure has played an important role in legislating for the increased participation of, and in some sports visibility of, women competitors. In the UK the 1975 Sexual Discrimination Act has enabled some legal challenges to discrimination in sport, but its effectivity in this area is limited because of a number of exemption clauses (Hargreaves 1994: 175–7).

While the success of women in the Olympics, basketball and soccer is often attributed to the piece of civil rights legislation Title IX, the ways in which this success is treated in some quarters is to assert that, because women are now visibly successful in sport, there is no further need for such legislation. Popular media representations of sportswomen are often linked to images of a variety of *fictional* 'ass-kicking babes' – Lara Croft, the Powerpuff Girls, Buffy the Vampire Slayer, the reinvented Charlie's Angels – in support of the argument that post-feminist femininity enables women to be both glamorous and aggressive (for example, Hill, 2001). In view of these developments, has there been any real increase in the representation of women in sport, and has its nature changed?

The Olympic Games is a crucial site for the issue of gender and sport. The founder of the modern Olympics and President of the International Olympic Committee from 1896 to 1925, Baron Pierre de Coubertin, based his whole philosophy of sport precisely on the exclusion of women. In the *Revue Olympique* in 1912 he restated his original formulation that the games should be about 'the solemn and periodic exaltation of male athleticism, based on internationalism, by means of fairness, in an artistic setting, with the applause of women as a reward' (de Coubertin, 2000: 731). In a speech in 1928, he was reported saying:

> The ruggedness of male exertion, the basis of athletic education when prudently but resolutely applied, is much to be dreaded when it comes to the female. That ruggedness is achieved physically only when nerves are stretched beyond their normal capacity, and morally only when the most precious feminine characteristics are nullified ... Add a female element, and the event becomes monstrous ... If some women want to play football or box, let them, provided that the event takes place without spectators, because the spectators who flock to such competitions are not there to watch a sport. (de Coubertin, 2000: 188–9)

Despite de Coubertin's outright opposition, and after exclusion from the first modern Olympics in 1896, women did participate in subsequent games. In 1900 ten women competed. Even by 1932 only 14 events were open to women, and 127 as opposed to 1281 men, took part. Women always constituted less than 10 per cent of the total number of participants for the first half of the twentieth century (Schaffer and Smith, 2000: 4).

At the centennial Olympics in Atlanta in 1996, women constituted a higher proportion of athletes competing than ever before, but this was still only 36 per cent. Research on gender issues of the Atlanta Olympics has proliferated (Andrews, 1998; Borcila, 2000; Chisholm, 1999; Eastman and Billings, 1999; Heywood, 2000; Tuggle and Owen, 1999), joining a tradition of previous analyses of gender at Olympic Games (Duncan, 1990; Toohey, 1997).

At first sight the Atlanta Games seemed to provide the arena for more 'assertive' representations of femininity. NBC explicitly targeted women in its 1996 Olympic coverage (Coakley, 1998: 214): 'the games of the woman'. Daddario (1998) argued that commercial sponsors were eager to develop a female audience through the use of storytelling techniques derived from soap opera. In Daddario's view, the logic of increasing commercialisation, the need for business to seek out untapped markets, will help to undermine the status of sport as a patriarchal preserve. And there have been few events as heavily watched as the showdown between Tonya Harding and Nancy Kerrigan at the 1994 Winter Olympics (Baughman, 1995).

Yet a number of studies have shown that media coverage of the Atlanta Olympics did not provide significant evidence of increased visibility for women, despite claims that this was the 'Games of the Woman' (Eastman and Billings, 1999), although within the overall imbalance of coverage there were some women's events that attracted significantly more attention. It should be noted, too, that while NBC were celebrating Atlanta as the 'Games of the Woman', only 11 of its 51 reporters and commentators were assigned to cover women's events and 'Despite increase of women athletes, most Olympic reporters are still men' (www.feminist.org 18 July 1996).

Media summaries of the Sydney Olympics in 2000 focused on that event as one in which women had been the stars. Take one piece in the *Observer,* headlined 'Sydney's Female Form'. This article asserts that Cathy Freeman's 400m and Marion Jones's thwarted quest to win 5 golds had been the performances of the games, easily outshining the men. A key theme in the article is that the increased performance of women athletes goes hand in hand with their increased glamorization. Like many other media reports, the *Observer* review reproduces a quote from pole vaulter Tatiana Grigorieva: 'They thought we boring. Now there are hot chicks clearing 15 feet, they want us.' Furthermore, the attitude of sportswomen is seen to be more appropriate to the Olympic ideal than that of sportsmen. The article compares the 'grouchy, sullen and aloof' attitude of the USA men's basketball 'Dream Team' with the Aussie women's water polo team.

This leads into another interesting theme of recent media representations: some women's sports are increasingly being represented as 'more enlightened, authentic and pure than men's sports' (Cole, 2000: 6). Tennis is one such sport, and the theme particularly suits the Olympics, with all the baggage that goes with the games. The showboating behaviour of the USA men's 4 × 100 relay team was compared unfavourably with that of the women's equivalent (see Chapter 7).

The women's soccer world cup in the United States in 1999 is also represented as an example of the development of women's sport: 'I've seen the future of football and the future is feminine,' said the FIFA President Sepp Blatter ('America's Rose Bowl sell-out', *news.bbc.co.uk*, 10 July 1999). The final at the LA Rose Bowl was attended by a crowd of around 90,000 to watch the United States beat China on penalties. The stars of the US team, such as their captain Mia Hamm, were heavily endorsed by Nike and Gatorade. And one of the most notable images from the tournament was when Brandi Chastain, after scoring the winning penalty, took off her shirt to reveal Nike's latest sports bra (an image which, inevitably, made the cover of *Sports Illustrated*) – a paradigmatic example of how post-feminism and commodification are interrelated.

Cole argues that Hamm's achievements represents a 'story that post-affirmative action America loves to tell itself about itself' (2000: 4):

> For ... America's Title IX generation, the gender gap has not
> only narrowed, but it's irrelevant. Hamm's achievements are
> women's achievements. Athletes are athletes. Women's sports
> are here to stay. Professional opportunities, television super-
> stars, high profile sporting events, announce the prominence
> and popularity of women's sports. (Cole, 2000: 4)

Along with Olympic sports and soccer, tennis is used to demonstrate the increasing significance of women's sport. Throughout
1999 an evolving soap opera unfolded in worldwide newspaper
coverage of women's tennis, usefully illustrating the complex ways
in which the media represents the development of women's sports.
On the one hand, the media represented women's tennis as epitomising the gains made by women in sport in general, citing as
evidence the growing power and athleticism of a new generation
of players, the growth of endorsements and increased visibility in
the media. On the other hand, the media represented these gains in
quite stereotypical ways, suggestive rather of continuity than of
transformation.

Connell (1987) argues that gender is a relational concept. This
does not just mean that masculinity is defined in relation to femininity and vice versa, but also that different definitions within femininity and masculinity are formed in relation to one another. The
women's tennis 'soap opera' featured a cast of characters epitomising
different definitions of femininity. Further, as with any long-running
soap opera, characters that feature in any given season signify in
terms of their similarities or differences with characters in previous
seasons.

The tennis year is based around the four grand slam events: 1999
started with a run to the final of the Australian Open of a player
largely unknown to the general public, Amelie Mauresmo, who had
publicly identified herself as a lesbian. When Martina Hingis
described her as 'half a man', and the defeated semi-finalist Lindsay
Davenport said, 'I mean, I thought I was playing a guy', the media
had a field day. Not only did these remarks validate one of the most
pervasive stereotypes affecting the representation of women in sport,

but the issue had been raised by women players, thus absolving the media from the responsibility for raising the stereotype. When the media had blown up these statements, Davenport threatened to withdraw cooperation with the press.

This incident provided the frame for the rest of the year's coverage: that women's tennis is increasingly dominated by more powerful players. An article in the *Guardian* (20 May 1999) succinctly summarises the ways in which the media in general began to represent the emergence of these players:

> Venus and Serena Williams, the American sisters built like rugby lock forwards, have been closely followed by Amelie Mauresmo, a woman with shoulders so broad she is rumoured to enter the locker room sideways ... ('The frill has gone')

And how had these physiques been achieved? In the case of former glamour girl Mary Pierce she had not only been working on her upper body strength during the close season but she had also been taking the legal muscle-building supplement, creatine.

Powerful women players were represented as having achieved their physique through unnatural means, reinforcing stereotypical definitions of 'natural' femininity.

The role of media sport in naturalising heterosexuality through linking 'mannishness' to lesbianism has been well researched (Cahn 1994, 1998; Wright and Clarke, 1999). Miller *et al.* (2001) argue that Mauresmo, rather than Pierce or the Williams sisters, bore the brunt of the criticism of mannish women tennis players because of her sexuality, just as Martina Navratilova and Renee Richards (Birrell and Cole, 1990) had done before. However, perhaps the homophobic media discourse is not that discriminating; in my reading of the media coverage Mauresmo and Pierce are often bracketed together, even though Pierce was within a heterosexual relationship at the time. Homophobic discourse functions to keep heterosexual men and women in line.

When the WTA circuit moved to the French Open, news coverage of the tournament was characterised by Martina Hingis's 'erratic' behaviour. Hingis was apparently unsettled by the adverse reaction of the crowd, ascribed in some press reports to her 'half a man' attack on their national hero Amelie Mauresmo at the Australian Open. In the final with Steffi Graf, Hingis lost a disputed line call, took a long toilet break in the middle of a game, in which she changed her dress, returned to serve underarm and then, to the crowd's astonishment, repeated it, and, having lost, had to be persuaded by her mother not to leave the court before the presentation ceremony. When it came to the third grand slam at Wimbledon, and Hingis lost to 16-year-old qualifier Jelena Dokic, the explanation was now that she had apparently banned her mother from watching. The *Daily Mail* announced Hingis's defeat with the headline, 'Where's mum when I need her?' (23 June 1999). This scenario dovetailed nicely with the stereotype of the emotionally vulnerable female tennis player (Hilliard, 1994), and also allowed rehearsal of the theme of female tennis players' relationships with their parents. This angle has been run on Steffi Graf, Mary Pierce, the Williams sisters and, most recently, Jelena Dokic.

Another favourite media issue that reached its height before and during Wimbledon was the question of unequal prize money between the men's and women's tournaments at three of the four Grand Slams (the US Open being the exception), with rumours of a planned strike. In the UK media this exploded when during an after-game press conference England's great white hope Tim Henman described women tennis players as 'greedy' for wanting equal prize money. Interestingly, the UK newspapers attacked him for this ('Intrigue continues to mount on a rainy day in England', *Washington Times*, 30 June 1999). The issue generated a whole range of articles about the glamour of women's tennis, particularly about how women tennis players such as Anna Kournikova could make more on sponsorship – over $10m a year – than the most successful men and women alike could make in prize money. Kournikova was depicted as the ideal means through which interest in the women's game as a whole could be stimulated. By implication, the more powerful players were represented as potentially putting sponsors off. A series of headlines in the *Daily Mail* provide good examples: 'Glamour's good; the women's game is booming; so it dare not let muscles muscle in and spoil our fun' (10 May 1999); 'Give me beauty not biceps, says Anna; Kournikova sticks to her guns over her bulging rivals' (28 May 1999); 'Court queens who defy the tennis terminators; we're the sporty spices, say Martina and Anna' (10 June 1999). Nevertheless although many newspapers proclaimed that either masculine or lesbian women tennis players were less likely to attract sponsorship, Amelie Mauresmo's agent was negotiating attractive sponsorship deals ('Amelie Mauresmo turns Aussie Open jeers to marketing and endorsement cheers' *Daily News* [New York], 7 February 1999).

Thus women's tennis illustrates the complex effects the increasing commodification of sport is having on the representation of gender. The increased role played by 'new entrants' into the field of media sport who define themselves in opposition to traditional sporting values and organisations has led to the expression of progressive messages around gender. Sports-related media have provided a vehicle for more assertive messages around femininity. As part of Nike's general rebelliousness, many of its ads have drawn on the language of 'popular feminism' (Cole and Hribar, 1995). There are limits, though, to the extent of Nike's advertisements in this respect. Firstly, the type of feminism it promotes is both consumerist and highly individualistic. It is not a feminism that encourages solidarity with other women (see also Lucas 2000; Goldman and Papson, 1998).

The advances made by women in sport with the help of legislation such as Title IX and the support of organisations such as the Women's Sports Foundation needs to be fully recognised. But at the same time the sports media's response has been equivocal. We read and hear that women's sport has arrived. Yet there is little evidence to suggest that the media is routinely covering women's sport *in general* any more than it has always done. Those stories that do surface on women's sport tend to reinforce its marginalisation through representing it as unusual. Further, where women's sport is represented sexualisation has if anything being given a new lease of life. A report produced by the Sports Sponsorship Advisory Service advised sportswomen to 'play the sex appeal card to attract more media coverage and therefore more sponsorship' (*Guardian* 26 August 1999).

Conclusion

This chapter has argued that in examining media sport's role in the reproduction of gender inequalities, the concepts of hegemonic masculinity and emphasised/hegemonic femininity are useful in a number of ways. Firstly, media representations of sport constitute a site where meanings around gender are continually contested, not fixed. The increased visibility of women in media coverage of some sports should not either be celebrated as evidence that women are approaching equality with men, or condemned as a patriarchal accommodation of women's sport. The concepts of hegemonic masculinity/emphasised femininity should provide a warning against exaggerating the significance of *spectacular* media representations of gender: either those of excessive male violence, such as associated with Mike Tyson, or of women's success at events like the women's soccer World Cup and the Olympics. The news value of such representations lies precisely in that they are dealing with something out of the ordinary. What is perhaps more telling is the banal, day-by-day drip feed of newspaper and television sports coverage which is still overwhelmingly about men, and naturalises the equation of sport with masculinity. Spectacular media sport representations have their place, but perhaps this is to throw into relief the everyday assumptions about gender that underpin most media coverage of sport and which come to be taken for granted. Finally, the concepts of hegemonic masculinity and emphasised femininity are based on a theory that stresses the interaction of gender with other social identities. Representations about gender are never solely about gender. The ways in which the media represents sportsmen and sportswomen in terms of masculinity and femininity is inextricably linked to the way in which they are represented in terms of their 'race', nation, class or sexuality.

|7|

Conclusion

The photograph on the cover of this book depicts an incident at the 2000 Sydney Olympics which epitomises the key themes discussed in this book: the mediatisation, globalisation and commodification of sport and the significance of these processes in terms of social identities based on the intersection of nation, race and gender.

The American 4 × 100 relay team celebrated their win with an extravagant and spectacular victory lap. Two of them had stripped their Nike unitards to the waist, and all of them strutted and postured for photographers using the stars and stripes as a prop. Pro wrestling fans would have recognised that team member Bernard Williams had deliberately adopted the 'people's eyebrow', the signature gesture of World Wrestling Federation superstar 'the Rock'. (Of course, the WWF is the antithesis of the Olympic ideal.)

Worse for the Olympic authorities, after former US Secretary of State Henry Kissinger had presented them with their medals, instead of standing to rapt attention during 'The Star-Spangled Banner' the foursome continued to clown about, according to press reports. Many newspapers commented on the particular inappropriateness of their behaviour given that it was performed in front of the senior international statesman.

Subsequently the team were attacked from all sides. The display earned a rebuke from Nanceen Perry on behalf of the women's 4 × 100 relay team for its lack of respect for the flag. The medallists immediately apologised. But it was too late to stop NBC and the rest of the US media condemning their behaviour, or to stop criticism from some members of the public. Team member Jon Drummond said he had received 125 to 200 e-mails a day in the two weeks following, most of them critical and many containing racist abuse. But the antics of the team were also compared unfavourably to the protest by John Carlos and Tommie Smith at the 1968 Mexico Olympics, who during the national anthem had lowered their heads and given the 'Black Power' salute, and who had been sent home as a consequence (see Chapter 5). At least Carlos and Smith were making a sincere, political gesture went the criticism, whereas today's foursome were just goofing around.

The team seemed genuinely bewildered at the response and explained that they were just expressing themselves in the way that came naturally and putting on a show for the crowd, that there was no intention to offend. For Williams, expressing themselves meant employing a pro wrestler's moves. And Maurice Greene later admitted that an Olympic win should not be celebrated in the same way as an end zone spike in football.

This incident illustrates the complexities and contradictions characterising global media sport discussed in this book. Firstly, there is the tension between the ideals of sport as legislated for by national and international non-governmental organisations, and the role of sport in providing an increasingly commodified spectacle for the global media. In this example the USATF headed off possible disciplinary action by the IOC by censuring the athletes and by promising to implement a code of conduct. Both organisations sought to discipline behaviour judged to undermine dominant conceptions of national identity. Yet the pictures of exorbitant and spectacular celebrations transmitted around the world are precisely what media companies would want of their sports stars, even if the commentators and journalists the latter employ simultaneously condemn the athlete's behaviour.

Then there is the matter of national identity – as the outcry was over the extent to which the athletes had been disrespectful to the nation through their behaviour. Here we see that representations of national identity in media sport are never just representations of national identity. The USATF and the IOC seek to discipline all athletes to behave the same way towards the flag, whatever the race, gender, class, or sexuality of the athlete. Any display which might disrupt the representation of sport as a symbol of national unification is condemned. In this case much of the criticism from the media and the public focused on the fact that the relay team were all African-Americans, with some media commentators arguing that the team were bad role models for the African-Americans, and members of the public expressing racist viewpoints. The fact that much of the media coverage represented the team as incapable of thinking through the implications of their behaviour doubtless reinforced a stereotypical view that would ascribe these athletes' achievement to 'natural' ability in speed events which don't require tactics or strategy – a stereotype originally underpinned by spurious scientific claims but upheld nowadays by an appeal to genetics.

But gender is also crucial to the representation of national identity. When it comes to sport playing a role in the construction of the nation it is almost always male team sports that are seen as the most important. Referring again to Williams' adoption of 'the Rock's' pose, here was an example of an athlete using poses and gestures associated with the cartoon hypermasculinity of professional wrestling with its choreographed violence. Whilst the other team members did not appear to have consciously adopted explicit wrestling references, the muscle flexing and posturing also belongs to that world. In their condemnation of such displays of hypermasculinity displayed by African-American sportsmen, media and sports organisations tend if in anything to reinforce hegemonic definitions of masculinity – the currently commonsense, taken for-granted, and therefore mostly silent definition of masculinity that tends to function in the interests of white, middle-class men (see Chapter 6).

And these celebrations were also explicitly juxtaposed with those performed by Cathy Freeman, winner of the 400 metres. Previously reprimanded (Commonwealth Games 1994) for waving the aboriginal flag with the Australian flag on her victory lap, the same gesture at the opening ceremony and in celebrating victory in her own event at the Sydney Olympics was accepted as a sign for the questionable claim that white Australia had become reconciled with its aboriginal population.

Reflecting on the episode and the outcry it provoked allows us to appreciate the complexities of researching and analysing media images of sport. It shows well the conflict between the Olympian ideal of sport and commercial, professional sport, and the ways in which definitions of nation, race and gender interact in quite complex ways.

The lesson of this and similar examples is that in applying concepts such as globalisation, commodification, nation, race and gender to the analysis of representation of sport in the media, need only to be critical about the way in which we do this, but also to examine the interplay of all of these concepts within *historically specific* cases.

References

Ahmed, K. (1998) Press warned to watch language in covering World Cup, *Guardian*, 14 May.

Anderson, B. (1991) *Imagined Communities* (2nd edn). London: Verso.

Andrews, D. (1996a) Deconstructing Michael Jordan: reconstructing post-industrial America. *Sociology of Sport Journal*, 13: 315–18.

— (1996b) Sport and the masculine hegemony of the modern nation: Welsh rugby, culture and society 1890–1914, in J. Nauright and T. Chandler (eds), *Making Men: Rugby and Masculine Identity*. London: Frank Cass.

— (1996c) The fact(s) of Michael Jordan's blackness: excavating a floating racial signifier. *Sociology of Sport Journal*, 13: 125–58.

— (1997) The (trans)national basketball association: American commodity–sign culture and global–local conjuncturalism, in A. Cvetkovich and D. Kellner (eds), *Articulating the Local and the Global: Globalization and Cultural Studies*. Boulder, CO: Westview.

— (1998) Feminizing Olympic reality. Preliminary dispatches from Baudrillard's Atlanta. *International Review for the Sociology of Sport*, 33(1): 5–18.

— B. Carrington, Jackson, S. and Mazur, Z. (1996) Jordanscapes: a preliminary analysis of the global popular. *Sociology of Sport Journal*, 13: 428–57.

Appadurai, A. (1995) Playing with modernity: the decolonisation of

Indian cricket, in C. Breckenridge (ed.), *Consuming Modernity: Public Culture in a South Asian World*. Minneapolis: University of Minnesota Press.

Bairner, A. (2001) *Sport, Nationalism and Globalization*. Albany: State University of New York Press.

Banet-Weiser, S. (1999) Hoop dreams: professional basketball and the politics of race and gender. *Journal of Sport and Social Issues*, 23(4): 403–20.

Barnett, S. (1990) *Games and Sets: The Changing Face of Sport on Television*. London: BFI.

— (1995) Sport, in A. Smith (ed.), *Television: an international history*. Oxford: Oxford University Press.

Barthes, R. (1973) *Mythologies*. London: Jonathan Cape.

Baughman, C. (ed.) (1995) *Women on Ice: Feminist Essays on the Tonya Harding/Nancy Kerrigan Spectacle*. New York: Routledge.

Bellamy, R. (1998) The evolving television sports marketplace, in L. Wenne (ed.), *MediaSport*. New York: Routledge.

Benedict, J. (1997) *Public Heroes, Private Felons: Athletes and Crimes against Women*. Boston: Northeastern University Press.

Benedict, J. and Yeager, D. (1998) *Pros and Cons: The Criminals who Play in the NFL*. New York: Warner.

Bernstein, A. (2000) 'Things you can see from there you can't see from here': globalization, media and the Olympics. *Journal of Sport and Social Issues*, 24(4): 351–69.

Billig, M. (1995) *Banal Nationalism*. London: Sage.

Birrell, S. and Cole, C. L. (1990) Double fault: Renée Richards and the construction and naturalization of difference. *Sociology of Sport Journal*, 7(1): 1–21.

Black, D. and Nauright, J. (1998) *Rugby and the South African Nation*. Manchester: Manchester University Press.

Blain, N. and Boyle, R. (1994) Battling along the boundaries, the marking of Scottish identity in sports journalism, in G. Jarvie and G. Walker (eds), *Scottish Sport in the Making of the Nation*. Leicester: Leicester University Press.

— and O'Donnell, H. (1993) *Sport and National Identity in the European Media*. Leicester: Leicester University Press.

Blain, N. and O'Donnell, H. (1998) European sports journalism and its readers during Euro '96: 'Living without the *Sun*', in M. Roche (ed.), *Sport, Popular Culture and Identity*. Aachen: Meyer & Meyer.

Booth, Douglas (1999) Recapturing the moment: global rugby, economics and the politics of nation in post-apartheid South Africa, in T. J. L. Chandler and J. Nauright (eds), *Making the Rugby World: Race, Gender, Commerce*. London: Frank Cass.

Borcila, A. (2000) Nationalizing the Olympics around and away from 'vulnerable' bodies of women. The NBC coverage of the 1996 Olympics and some moments after. *Journal of Sport and Social Issues*, 24(2): 118–47.

Bourgeois, N. (1995) Sports journalists and their source of information: a conflict of interests and its resolution. *Sociology of Sport Journal*, 12(2): 195–203.

Boutilier, M. A. and SanGiovanni, L. F. (1994) Politics, public policy and title IX: some limitations of liberal feminism, in S. Birrell and C. L. Cole (eds), *Women, Sport and Culture*. Champaign: Human Kinetics.

Boyd, T. (1997) The day the niggaz took over: basketball, commodity culture and black masculinity, in A. Baker and T. Boyd (eds), *Out of Bounds. Sports, Media and the Politics of Identity*. Bloomington: Indiana University Press.

Boyle, R. and Haynes, R. (1996) 'The grand old game': football, media and identity in Scotland. *Media Culture and Society*, 18: 549–64.

—(2000) *PowerPlay: Sport, the Media and Popular Culture*. London: Longman.

Brackenridge, C. (1997) 'He owned me basically': women's experience of sexual abuse in sport. *International Review for the Sociology of Sport*, 32(2): 115–30.

Brookes, R. (1998) Time, national identity and television schedules in the 'postbroadcast age'. *Time and Society*, 7(2): 369–81.

—(1999) Newspaper and national identities: the BSE/CJD crisis and the British press. *Media, Culture and Society*, 21: 247–63.

Brown, A. and Walsh, A. (1999) *Not for Sale. Manchester United, Murdoch and the Defeat of BSkyB*. London: Mainstream.

Bryant, J. (1989) Viewers enjoyment of televised sports violence, in L. Wenner (ed), *Media, Sports and Society*. Newbury Park, CA: Sage.

Cahn, S. (1994) *Coming on Strong: Gender and Sexuality in Twentieth-Century Women's Sport*. Cambridge, MA: Harvard University Press.

— (1998) From the 'muscle moll' to the 'butch' ballplayer: mannishness: lesbianism and homophobia in US women's sport. *Feminist Studies*, 19(2): 343–68.

Carrington, B. (1998) 'Football's coming home', but whose home? and do we want it?: nation, football and the politics of exclusion, in A. Brown (ed.), *Fanatics! Power, Identity and Fandom in Football*. London: Routledge.

Cashmore, E. (1997) *The Black Cultural Industry*. London: Routledge.

— (1999) Women's greatest handicaps: sex, medicine, and men. *British Journal of Sports Medicine*, 33: 76–7.

— (2000) *Sports Culture: An A-Z Guide*. London: Routledge.

Chaudhary, V. (2000) FIFA mix-up over 2006 bid threats. *Guardian*, 8 July.

Chisholm, A. (1999) Defending the nation: national bodies, US borders, and the 1996 US Olympics women's gymnastics team. *Journal of Sport and Social Issues*, 23: 126–39.

Coakley, J. (1998) *Sport in Society. Issues and Controversies* (6th edn). Maidenhead, Berkshire: McGraw Hill.

Cole, C. L. (1996) American Jordan: P.L.A.Y., consensus, and punishment. *Sociology of Sport Journal*, 13: 366–97.

— (2000) The year that girls ruled. *Journal of Sports and Social Issues*, 24(1): 3–7.

— and Andrews, D. (2000) America's new son: Tiger Woods and America's multiculturalism, in N. Denzin (ed.), *Cultural Studies: A Research Volume*, vol. 5. Stamford: JAI Press.

— and Denny, H. (1995) Visualising deviance in post-Reagan America: Magic Johnson, AIDS, and the promiscuous world of professional sport. *Critical Sociology* 20(3): 123–47.

— and Hribar, A. (1995) Celebrity feminism: Nike style. Post-Fordism, transcendence and consumer power. *Sociology of Sport Journal*, 12: 347–69.

Collier, G. (2000) I was looking for heroes in all the wrong places. *Columbia Journalism Review*, 38, Jan–Feb, 48–9.

Connell, R. (1987) *Gender and Power*. Cambridge: Polity.

— (1990) An iron man: the body and some contradictions of hegemonic masculinity, in M. Messner and D. Sabo (eds), *Sport, Media and the Gender Order*. Champaign, IL: Human Kinetics.

— (1995) *Masculinities*. Cambridge: Polity.

Coubertin, P. de. (2000) *Olympism: Selected Writings,* ed. N. Miller. Lausanne: International Olympic Committee.

Crawford, S. (1999) Nelson Mandela, the number 6 jersey, and the 1995 Rugby World Cup: sport as a transcendent unifying force, or a transparent illustration of bicultural opportunism, in R. Sands (ed.), *Anthropology, Sport and Culture*. Westport, CT: Bergin & Garvey.

Creeber, G. (ed.) (2001) *The television genre book*. London: BFI.

Creedon, P. (1994) Women in toyland: a look at women in American newspaper sports journalism, in P. Creedon (ed.), *Women, Media and Sport*. Thousand Oaks, CA: Sage.

Critcher, C. (1994) England and the World Cup: World Cup willies, English football and the myth of 1966, in J. Sugden and A. Tomlinson (eds), *Hosts and Champions: Soccer Cultures, National Identities and the USA World Cup*. Aldershot: Arena.

Curran, J. and Sparks, C. (1991) Press and popular culture. *Media, Culture and Society* 13(2): 215–37.

Curran, J., Douglas, A. and Whannel, G. (1980) The political economy of the human interest story, in A. Smith (ed.), *Newspapers and Democracy*. Cambridge, MA: MIT Press.

Daddario, G. (1998) Women's sport and spectacle: gendered television coverage and the Olympic Games. Westport, CT: Praeger.

Davies, D. (1999) Tiger's treasure Nike pays Woods record-breaking $90m to sport the swoosh – and nothing else. *Guardian*, 25 August.

Davis, L. R. (1990) The articulation of difference: White preoccupation with the question of racially linked genetic differences among athletes. *Sociology of Sport Journal*, (7): 179–87.

— (1997) *The Swimsuit Issue and Sport: Hegemonic Masculinity in Sports Illustrated*. Albany, NJ: State University of New York Press.

Dayan, D. and Katz, E. (1992) *Media Events. The Live Broadcasting of History*. Cambridge: Harvard University Press.

Denzin, N. (1996) More rare Air: Michael Jordan on Michael Jordan. *Sociology of Sport Journal*, 13: 319–24.

Dodson, S. and Barkham, P. (2000) Why the net is not invited to Sydney. *Online Guardian*, 14 Sept: 2–3.

Donald, J. and Rattansi, A. (1992) Introduction, in J. Donald and A. Rattansi (eds), *'Race', culture and difference*. London: Sage.

Donnelly, P. (1996) The local and the global: globalization in the sociology of sport. *Journal of Sport and Social Issues*, 20(3): 239–57.

Duke, V. and Crolley, L. (1996) *Football, Nationality and the State*. London: Longman.

Dunbar, M. D. (2000) Do you feel feminine yet? Black masculinity, gender transgression, and reproductive rebellion on MTV, in J. McKay, M. A. Messner and D. Sabo (eds), *Masculinities, Gender Relations and Sport*. London: Sage.

Duncan, M. C. (1990) Sports photographs and sexual difference: images of women and men in the 1984 and 1988 Olympic Games. *Sociology of Sport Journal*, 7: 22–43.

— Messner, M.A., Williams, L. and Jensen, K. (1994) Gender stereotyping in televised sports (ed. W. Wilson), in S. Birrell and C. L. Cole (eds), *Women, Sport and Culture*. Champaign: Human Kinetics.

Dunning, E. (1999) *Sport Matters*. London: Routledge.

— and Sheard, K. (1979) *Barbarians, Gentlemen and Players: A Sociological Study of the Development of Rugby Football*. Oxford: Martin Robertson.

— Maguire, J. and Pearton, R. (1993) Introduction, in E. Dunning, J. Maguire and R. Pearton (eds), *The Sports Process: A Comparative and Developmental Approach*. Champaign, IL: Human Kinetics.

Dworkin, S. L. and Wachs, F. L. (1998) 'Disciplining the body': HIV-positive male athletes, media surveillance, and the policing of sexuality, *Sociology of Sport Journal*, 15: 1–20.

— (2000) The morality/manhood paradox: masculinity, sport and the media, in J. McKay, M. Messner and D. Sabo (eds), *Masculinities, Gender Relations and Sport*. London: Sage.

Eastman, S. T. and Billings, A. (1999) Gender parity in the Olympics. Hyping women athletes, favoring men athletes. *Journal of Sport and Social Issues*, 23(2): 140–70.

— (2000) Sportscasting and sports reporting. The power of gender bias. *Journal of Sport and Social Issues*, 24(2): 192–213.

Eastman, S. T. and Riggs, K. E. (1994) Televised sports and ritual: fan experiences. *Sociology of Sport Journal*, 11: 249–74.

Elias, N. (1986) The genesis of sport as a sociological problem, in N. Elias and E. Dunning (eds), *Quest for Excitement: Sport and Leisure in the Civilising Process*. Oxford: Blackwell.

Evans, J., Davies, B. and Bass, D. (1999) More than a game: physical culture, identity and citizenship in Wales, in G. Jarvie (ed.), *Sport in the Making of Celtic Cultures*. Leicester: Leicester University Press.

Farred, G. (1997) The nation in white: cricket in a post apartheid South Africa. *Social Text*, 15(1): 9–32.

Fiske, J. (1987) *Television Culture*. London: Routledge.

— (1989) *Understanding Popular Culture*. Unwin & Hyman.

Frith, S. (1996) Entertainment, in J. Curran and M. Gurevitch (eds), *Mass Media and Society*. (2nd edn). London: Arnold.

Gantz, W. and Wenner, L. (1995) Fanship and the Television Sports Viewing Experience, *Sociology of Sport Journal*, 12: 56–74.

Garland, J. and Rowe, M. (1999) War minus the shooting? Jingoism, the English press and Euro '96. *Journal of Sport and Social Issues*, 23(1): 80–95.

Garrison, B. and Salwen, M. (1989) Newspaper sports journalists: a profile of the profession. *Journal of Sport and Social Issues*, 13(2): 57–68.

— (1994) Sports journalists assess their work: their place in the profession. *Newspaper Research Journal*, 15(2): 37–49.

Geertz, C. (1973) *The Interpretation of Cultures*. New York: Basic Books.

Gerbner, G. (1978) The dynamics of cultural resistance, in G. Tuchman, A. K. Daniels and J. Benet (eds), *Hearth and Home: Images of Women in the Mass Media*. New York: Oxford University Press.

Giddens, A. (1990) *The Consequences of Modernity*. Cambridge: Polity.

Gilroy, P. (2000) *Between Camps. Race, Identity and Nationalism at the End of the Colour Line*. London: Allen Lane.

Giulianotti, R. (1999) *Football: A Sociology of the Global Game*. Cambridge: Polity.

Goldlust, J. (1987) *Playing for keeps: sport, the media and society*. Melbourne: Longman Cheshire.

Goldman, R. and Papson, S. (1998) *Nike Culture*. London: Sage.

Gordon, S. and Sibson, R. (1998) Global television: the Atlanta Olympics opening ceremony, in D. Rowe and G. Lawrence (eds), *Tourism, Leisure, Sport: Critical Perspectives*. Sydney: Hodder.

Gruneau, R. (1989) Making spectacle: a case study in television sports production, in L. Wenner (ed.), *Media, Sports and Society*. Newbury Park, CA: Sage.

— and Whitson, D. (1993) *Hockey Night in Canada*. Toronto: Garamond.

Guttmann, A. (1991) Sports diffusion: a response to Maguire and the Americanization commentaries. *Sociology of Sport Journal*, 8:185–90.

— (1993) The diffusion of sports and the problem of cultural imperialism, in E. Dunning, J. Maguire and R. Pearton (eds), *The Sports Process*. Champaign, IL: Human Kinetics.

— (1994) *Games and Empires: Modern Sports and Cultural Imperialism*. New York: Columbia University Press.

Hall, S. (1990) The whites of their eyes: racist ideologies and the media, in M. Alvarado and J. O. Thompson (eds), *The Media Reader*. London: BFI.

— (1991a) The local and the global: globalization and ethnicity, in A. King (ed.), *Culture, Globalization and the World-System*. London: Macmillan.

— (1991b) Old and new identities, old and new ethnicities, in A. King (ed.), *Culture, Globalization and the World-System*. London: Macmillan.

— (1992) The question of cultural identity, in S. Hall, D. Held and T. McGrew (eds), *Modernity and its Futures*. Cambridge: Polity.

— (1996) What is this 'black' in black popular culture? in D. Morley and K.-H. Chen (eds), *Stuart Hall. Critical Dialogues in Cultural Studies*. London: Routledge.

Hardt-Mautner, G. (1995) 'How does one become a good European?': the British press and European integration. *Discourse and Society*, 6 (2): 177–205.

Hargreaves, Jennifer (1994) *Sporting Females*. London: Routledge.

Harvey, J. and Houle, F. (1994) Sport, world economy, global culture and new social movements. *Sociology of Sport Journal*, 11: 337–55.

— Rail, G. and Thibault, L. (1996) Globalization and sport. Sketching a theoretical model for empirical analysis. *Journal of Sport and Social Issues*, 20(3): 258–77.

Held, D., McGrew, A., Goldblatt, D. and Perraton, J. (1999) *Global Transformations*. Cambridge: Polity.

Heywood, L. (2000) The Girls of Summer: social contexts for the year of the woman at the '96 Olympics, in K. Shaffer and S. Smith (eds), *The Olympics at the Millennium*. Piscataway, NJ: Rutgers University Press.

Higgs, D. T. and Weiller, K. H. (1994) Gender bias and the 1992 Summer Olympic Games: an analysis of television coverage. *Journal of Sport and Social Issues*, 18: 234–46.

Hill, A. (2001) Women's knockout blow. *Observer*, 1 April.

Hill, C. (1993) The politics of the Olympic movement, in L. Allison (ed.), *The Changing Politics of Sport*. Manchester: Manchester University Press.

Hilliard, D. C. (1994) Televised sport and the (anti) sociological imagination. *Journal of Sport and Social Issues*, 18: 88–99.

Hirst, P. and Thompson, K. (1996) *Globalization in Question*. Cambridge: Polity.

Hoberman, J. (1997) *Darwin's Athletes: How Sport has damaged Black America and preserved the Myth of Race*. New York: Mariner.

Hobsbawm, E. (1990) *Nations and Nationalism since 1780*. Cambridge: Cambridge University Press.

Holland, P. (1997) *The Television Handbook*. London: Routledge.

Horne, J., Tomlinson, A. and Whannel, G. (1999) *Understanding Sport*. London: E & FN Spon.

Hoskins, C., McFadyen, S. and Finn, A. (1997) *Global Television and Film: An Introduction to the Economics of the Business.* Oxford: Oxford University Press.

Houlihan, B. (1994) Homogenization, Americanization, and Creolization of sport: varieties of globalization. *Sociology of Sport Journal*, 11: 356–75.

Ismail, Q. (1997) Batting against the break. On cricket, nationalism and the swashbuckling Sri Lankans. *Social Text*, 15(1): 33–56.

Jackson, S. (1998) A twist of race: Ben Johnson and the Canadian crisis of racial and national identity. *Sociology of Sport Journal*, 15(1): 21–40.

— and Andrews, D. (1999a) Between and beyond the global and the local: American popular sporting culture in New Zealand. *International Review for the Sociology of Sport*, 34(1): 31–42.

— (1999b) The globalist of them all: the 'everywhere man' Michael Jordan and American popular culture in postcolonial New Zealand, in R. Sands (ed.), *Anthropology, Sport and Culture.* Westport, CT: Bergin & Garvey.

— and Meier, K. (1999) Hijacking the hyphenated signifier: Donovan Bailey and the politics of racial and national identity in Canada, in R. Sands (ed.), *Anthropology, Sport and Culture.* Westport, CN: Bergin & Garvey.

James, C. L. R. (1963) *Beyond a Boundary.* New York: Pantheon.

Jansen, S. and Sabo, D. (1994) The sport/war metaphor: hegemonic masculinity, the Persian Gulf War, and the New World Order. *Sociology of Sport Journal*, 11: 1–17.

— (2000) *Inside the Olympic Industry.* Albany: State University of New York Press.

Jenkins, H. (1997) 'Never trust a snake': WWF wrestling as masculine melodrama, in A. Baker and T. Boyd (eds), *Out of Bounds: Sports, Media and the Politics of Identity.* Bloomington: Indiana University Press.

Jennings, A and Wilson, N. (2001) A tale of greed and the men who sold the world cup. www.soccernet.com 20 April.

Jhally, S. (1989) Cultural Studies and the sports/media complex, in L.

Wenner (ed.), *Media, Sports and Society*. Newbury Park, CA: Sage.

— and J. Lewis (1992) *Enlightened Racism: The Cosby Show, Audiences and the Myth of the American Dream*. Boulder, CO: Westview.

Johnson, L. and Roediger, D. (1997) 'Hertz, don't it?' Becoming colorless and staying black in the crossover of O. J. Simpson', in T. Morrison and C. B. Lacour (eds), *Birth of a Nation'hood*. New York: Pantheon.

Kane, M. J. and Disch, L. J. (1993) Sexual violence and the reproduction of male power in the locker room: the 'Lisa Olson incident', *Sociology of Sport Journal* 10: 331–52.

— and Greendorfer, S. L. (1994) The media's role in accommodating and resisting stereotyped images of women in sport, in P. Creedon (ed.), *Women, Media and Sport*. Thousand Oaks, CA: Sage.

Kellner, D. (1996) Sports, media culture and race – some reflections on Michael Jordan. *Sociology of Sport Journal*, 13: 458–67.

King, S. (1993) The politics of the body and the body politic: Magic Johnson and the ideology of AIDS. *Sociology of Sport Journal*. 10: 270–85.

Klein, A. (1991) Sport and culture as contested terrain: Americanization in the Caribbean. *Sociology of Sport Journal*, 8: 79–85.

Koranteng, J. (1998) *European Sports TV Channels*. London: FT Media and Telecoms.

LaFrance, M. and Rail, G. (2001) 'As bad as he says he is?' Interrogating Dennis Rodman's subversive potential, in S. Birrell and M. McDonald (eds), *Reading Sport*. Boston: Northwestern University Press.

Lash, S. and Urry, J. (1994) *Economies of Signs and Space*. London: Sage.

Lowes, M. (1997) Sports page: a case study in the manufacture of sports news for the daily press. *Sociology of Sport Journal*, 14: 143–59.

— (1999) *Inside the Sports Pages: Work Routines, Professional Ideologies and the Manufacture of Sports News*. Toronto: University of Toronto Press.

Lucas, S. (2000) Nike's commercial solution. Girls, sneakers and salvation. *International Review for the Sociology of Sport*, 35(2): 149–64.

Lule, J. (1995) The rape of Mike Tyson: race, the press and symbolic types. *Critical Studies in Mass Communication*, 12: 176–95.

McArthur, C. (1975) Setting the scene: Radio Times and TV Times, in Buscombe, E. (ed.), *Football on Television*. London: BFI.

McDonald, I. and Ugra, S. (1999) It's just not cricket ! Ethnicity, division and imagining the other in English cricket, in P. Cohen (ed.), *New Ethnicities,Old Racisms*. London: Zed.

McDonald, M. (1999) Unnecessary roughness: gender and racial politics in domestic violence media events. *Sociology of Sport Journal*, 16: 111–33.

— (2000) The marketing of the women's national basketball association and the making of postfeminism. *International Review for the Sociology of Sport*, 35(1): 35–47.

McKay, J. (1995) 'Just do it': Corporate slogans and the political economy of 'enlightened racism'. *Discourse Studies in the Cultural Politics of Education*, 16(2): 191–201.

— and Miller, T. (1991) From old boys to men and women of the corporation: the Americanization and commodification of Australian sport. *Sociology of Sport Journal*, 8: 86–94.

— and Smith, P. (1995) Exonerating the hero. Frames and narratives in media coverage of the O. J. Simpson story. *Media Information Australia*, 75: 57–66.

McLuhan, M. and Fiore, Q. (1967) *War and Peace in the Global Village*. New York: Bantam.

McNamara, T. (2000) 'You're a dumb broad' – and that's progress. *Columbia Journalism Review*. January-February: 43.

MacNeill, M. (1996) Networks: producing Olympic ice hockey for a national television audience. *Sociology of Sport Journal*, 13: 103–24.

Madan, M. (2000) 'It's not just cricket' World series cricket: race, nation and diasporic Indian identity. *Journal of Sport and Social Issues*, 24(1): 24–35.

Maguire, J. (1990) More than a sporting touchdown: the making of

American football in England, 1982–1990. *Sociology of Sport Journal*, 7: 213–37.

— (1993a) American football, British society and global sport development, in E. Dunning, J. Maguire and R. Pearton (eds), *The Sports Process*. Champaign, IL: Human Kinetics.

— (1993b) Globalisation, Sport and National Identities: 'The Empires Strikes Back'? *Society and Leisure*, 16(2): 293–322.

— (1994) Sport, identity politics and globalization: diminishing contrasts and increasing varieties, *Sociology of Sport Journal*, 11: 398–427.

— Poulton, E. and Possamai, C. (1999a) The war of the words? Identity politics in Anglo-German press coverage of Euro '96. *European Journal of Communication*, 14(1): 61–89.

— (1999b) Weltkreig III Media coverage of England versus Germany in Euro '96. *Journal of Sport and Social Issues*, 23(4): 439–44.

Malcolmson, R. (1982) Popular recreations under attack, in B. Waites, T. Bennett and G. Martin (eds), *Popular Culture: Past and Present*. London: Croom Helm/Open University Press.

Mayeda, D. T. (1999) From model minority to economic threat: media portrayals of Major League Baseball pitchers Hideo Nomo and Hideki Irabu. *Journal of Sport and Social Issues*, 23(2): 203–17.

Mee, B. (2000) Tyson serves up another freak show. *Daily Telegraph*, 26 June.

Mercer, C. (1992) 'Regular imaginings: the newspaper and the nation', in T. Bennett, P. Buckridge, D. Carter and C. Mercer (eds), *Celebrating the Nation* (Sydney: Allen & Unwin).

— Duncan, M. C. and Jensen, K. (1993) Separating the men from the girls: the gendered language of television sports. *Gender and Society*, 7(1): 121–37.

— Dunbar, M. and Hunt, D. (2000) The televised sports manhood formula. *Journal of Sport and Social Issues*, 24(4): 380–94.

— and Solomon, W. (1993) Outside the frame: newspaper coverage of the Sugar Ray Leonard wife abuse story. *Sociology of Sport Journal*, 10: 119–34.

Messner, M., Duncan, M. and Jensen, K. (1993) Separating the men from the girls: the gendered language of television sports. *Gender and Society*, 7(1): 121–37.

Meyrowitz, J. (1985) *No Sense of Place*. New York: Oxford University Press.

— and McHoul, A. (1998) *Popular Culture and Everyday Life*. London and Thousand Oaks, CA: Sage.

— Lawrence, G., McKay, J. and Rowe, D. (2001) *Globalization and Sport*. London: Sage.

Mitchell, K and Brooks, R. (1998) How C4 hit BBC for six. *Observer*, 18 October.

Nauright, J. (1997) *Sport, Culture and Identities in South Africa*. Leicester: Leicester University Press.

Nowell-Smith, G. (1979) Television – football – the world, *Screen* 19(4): 45–59.

O'Donnell, H. (1994) Mapping the mythical: a geopolitics of national sporting stereotypes, *Discourse and Society*, 5(3): 345–80.

Ohmae, K. (1990) *The Borderless World*. London: Collins.

Plaschke, B. (2000) The reporter: 'that's twice you get me. I'm gonna hit you, right now, right now!' *Columbia Journalism Review*, Jan–Feb: 42–4.

Polley, M. (1998) *Moving the Goalposts: A History of Sport and Society since 1945*. London: Routledge.

Polunbaum, J. and Wieting, S. G. (1999) Stories of sport and the moral order: unravelling the cultural construction of Tiger Woods. *Journalism and Communication Monographs*, 2(2): 69–108.

Real, M. (1975) The Super Bowl: mythic spectacle. *Journal of Communication*, 25(1): 31–43.

— (1989) Super Bowl football versus World Cup soccer: a cultural-structural comparison, in L. Wenner (ed.), *Media, Sports and Society*. Newbury Park: Sage.

Real, M. and Mechikoff, M. (1992) Deep fan: mythic identification, technology and advertising in spectator sports. *Sociology of Sports Journal*, 9: 323–39.

Review symposium (1998a) Review symposium on Davis (1997) *International Review for the Sociology of Sport*, 33(2): 189–203.

Review symposium (1998b) Review symposium on Hoberman (1997). *International Review for the Sociology of Sport*, 33(1): 83–99.

Robertson, R. (1990) Mapping the global condition, in M. Featherstone (ed.), *Global Culture*. London: Sage.

Rodman, D. and Keown, T. (1997) *Bad as I wanna be*. New York: Dell.

Rowe, D. (1994) Accommodating bodies: celebrity, sexuality and 'tragic magic'. *Journal of Sport and Social Issues*, 18(1): 6–26.

— (1996) The global love-match: sport and television. *Media, Culture and Society*, 18: 565-582.

— (1997) Apollo undone: the sports scandal, in J. Lull and S. Hinerman (eds), *Media Scandals: Morality and Desire in the Popular Culture Marketplace*. Cambridge: Polity.

— (1999) *Sport, Culture and the Media*. Buckingham: Open University Press.

— and D. Stevenson (1995) Negotiations and mediations: journalism, professional status and the making of the sports text. *Media Information Australia*, 75: 67–79.

— Lawrence, G., Miller, T. and McKay, J. (1994) Global sport? Core concern and peripheral vision. *Media, Culture and Society*, 16: 661–75.

Sabo, D., Gray, P. M. and Moore, L.A. (2000) Domestic violence and televised athletic events: 'It's a man thing', in J. McKay, M. Messner and D. Sabo (eds), *Masculinities, Gender Relations and Sport*. London: Sage.

Salwen, M. and Garrison, B. (1998) Finding their place in journalism: newspaper sports journalists' 'professional problems'. *Journal of Sport and Social Issues*, 22(1): 88–102.

Schaffer, K. and Smith, S. (eds) (2000) The games at the millennium, in *The Olympics at the Millennium*. Piscataway, NJ: Rutgers University Press.

Schwartz, D. (1997) *Contesting the Super Bowl*, New York: Routledge.

Serafini, D. (2000) SPORTEL claims monopoly of sports TV trade shows. www.VideoAgeInternational.com November.

Shilbury, D., Quick, S. and Westerbeek, H. (1998) *Strategic Sports Marketing*. Sydney: Allen & Unwin.

Shropshire, K. and Smith, E. (1998) The Tarzan syndrome. John

Hoberman and his quarrels with African American athletes and intellectuals. *Journal of Sport and Social Issues*, 22(1): 103–112.

Simons, L. M. (1999) Follow the ball. *American Journalism Review*. November 21(9): 69–73.

Sloop, J. (1997) Mike Tyson and the perils of discursive constraints: boxing, race and the assumption of guilt, in A. Baker and T. Boyd (eds), *Out of Bounds: Sports, Media and the Politics of Identity*. Bloomington: Indiana University Press.

Sreberny-Mohammadi, A. (2000) The global and the local in international communications, in J. Curran and M. Gurevitch (eds), *Mass Media and Society* (3rd edn). London: Arnold.

Sugden, J. and Tomlinson, A. (1998) *FIFA and the Contest for World Football*. Cambridge: Polity.

Theberge, N. and Cronk, A. (1986) Work routines in newspaper sports departments and the coverage of women's sports. *Sociology of Sport Journal*, 3: 195–203.

Tomlinson, A. (1996) Olympic spectacle: opening ceremonies and some paradoxes of globalization, *Media Culture and Society*, 18: 583–602.

— (2000) Carrying the torch for whom? Symbolic power and Olympic ceremony, in K. Schaffer and S. Smith (eds), *The Olympics at the Millennium*. Piscataway, NJ: Rutgers University Press.

Toohey, K. (1997) Australian television, gender and the Olympic Games. *International Review for the Sociology of Sport*, 32(1): 19–29.

Tracey, M. (1988) Popular culture and the economics of global television. *Intermedia*, 16(2): 8–25.

Trujillo, N. (1990) Hegemonic masculinity on the mound: media representations of Nolan Ryan and American sports culture. *Critical Studies in Mass Communication*, 8: 280–308.

— (1995) Machines, missiles and men: images of the male body on ABC's Monday Night Football. *Sociology of Sport Journal*, 12: 403–23.

Tudor, A. (1975) The panels, in E. Buscombe (ed.), *Football on Television*. London: BFI.

— (1992) Them and us: story and stereotype in TV world cup coverage. *European Journal of Communication*, 7: 391–413.

— (1998) Sports reporting: race, difference and identity, in K. Brants, J. Hermes and L. van Zoonen (eds), *The Media in Question*. London: Sage.

Tuggle, C. and Owen, A. (1999) A descriptive analysis of NBC's coverage of the centennial Olympics: the 'Games of the Woman'? *Journal of Sport and Social Issues*, 23(2): 171–82.

Tunstall, J. (1993) *Television Producers*. London: Routledge.

Tunstall, J. (1996) *Newspaper Power*. Oxford: Oxford University Press.

Tuohey, C. (1999) The Olberman factor. *American Journalism Review*, May 21(4): 38–42.

Volkwein, K., F. Schnell, A. Livezey and D. Sherwood (1997) Sexual harassment in sport: perceptions and experiences of American female student-athletes. *International Review for the Sociology of Sport*, 32(3): 283–96.

Wagg, S. (1991) Playing the past: the media and the England football team, in J. Williams and S. Wagg (eds), *British Football and Social Change: Getting into Europe*. Leicester: Leicester University Press.

Wagner, E. A. (1990) Sport in Asia and Africa: Americanization or mundialization? *Sociology of Sport Journal*, 7: 399–402.

Waters, M. (1995) *Globalization*. London: Routledge.

Watts, J. (1998) Soccer shinhatsubai: What are Japanese consumers making of the J. League, in D. P. Martinez (ed.), *The Worlds of Japanese Popular Culture*. Cambridge University Press.

Wenner, L. (1989) The Super Bowl pregame show: cultural fantasies and political subtext, in L. Wenner (ed.), *Media, Sports and Society*. Newbury Park: Sage.

— (1995) The good, the bad and the ugly: race, sport and the public eye. *Journal of Sport and Social Issues*, 19: 227–31.

— and W. Gantz (1989) The audience experience with sports on television, in L. Wenner (ed.), *Media, Sports and Society*. Newbury Park, CA: Sage.

Whannel, G. (1992) *Fields in Vision: Television Sport and Cultural Transformation*. London: Routledge.

Whiting, R. (1977) *The Chrysanthemum and the Bat*. New York: Avon.

Whitson, D. (1998) Circuits of promotion: media, marketing and the globalization of sport, in L. Wenner (ed.), *MediaSport*. New York: Routledge.

Williams, J. and Woodhouse, J. (1991) Can play, will play? Women and football in Britain, in J. Williams and S. Wagg (eds), *British Football and Social Change: Getting into Europe*. Leicester: Leicester University Press.

Wilson, B. (1997) 'Good blacks' and 'bad blacks': media constructions of African-American athletes in Canadian basketball. *International Review for the Sociology of Sport*, 32(2): 177–89.

Wren-Lewis, J. and Clarke, A. (1983) The World Cup – a political football. *Theory, Culture and Society*, 1(3): 123–32.

Wright, J. and Clarke, G. (1999) Sport, the media and the construction of compulsory heterosexuality: a case study of women's Rugby Union. *International Review for the Sociology of Sport*, 34(3): 227–43.

Index